YOUNG INDIA

YOUNG INDIA

AN INTERPRETATION AND A HISTORY OF THE NATIONALIST MOVEMENT FROM WITHIN

LAJPAT RAI

GYAN

Published by

Gyan Publishing House
5, Ansari Road
Daryaganj, New Delhi-110002
Phone: 011-47034999, 9811692060
E-mail: books@gyanbooks.com

Distribution Network
gyanbooks.com
India, USA, Canada, UK, Australia, France

ISBN: 978-81-212-7999-4 (PB)
First Published, 1916

2nd Impression 2023

Printed at: Gyan Press, Delhi.

YOUNG INDIA
Author: LAJPAT RAI

YOUNG INDIA

BY THE SAME AUTHOR

AN ECONOMIC HISTORY OF BRITISH INDIA

DADABHAI NAOROJI

YOUNG INDIA

AN INTERPRETATION AND A HISTORY OF THE NATIONALIST MOVEMENT FROM WITHIN

LAJPAT RAI

FOREWORD BY J. T. SUNDERLAND

ILLUSTRATED

"The people of India are capable of administering their own affairs and the municipal feeling is deep rooted in them. The village communities, each of which is a little republic, are the most abiding of Indian institutions."
(LORD LAWRENCE, once Viceroy and Governor-General of British India).

NEW YORK
B. W. HUEBSCH
1917

DEDICATED

TO

THE MEMORY OF MY DEAREST FRIEND

THE LATE LAMENTED

DWARKA DASS, M. A. OF THE PUNJAB

WHO DIED OF A BROKEN HEART, AT THE

COLLAPSE OF PUBLIC LIFE IN

HIS NATIVE PROVINCE,

(OCTOBER 1912)

AS AN HUMBLE TRIBUTE TO HIS UNCOMPROMISING

ATTITUDE TOWARDS PUBLIC LIFE, HIS

LOFTY PRINCIPLES, AND HIS NOBLE

ADVOCACY OF THEM

FOREWORD

Mr. Lajpat Rai, the author of this book, is one of the most widely known, most honoured and most influential public men in India. For more than twenty years he has been a leading member of the bar in Lahore, the capital city of the large province of the Punjab, and has long been prominent in public affairs both local and national.

From almost the beginning of the National Indian Congress he has been an active leader in that body, which is the most important political organization in the country. The last time I was in India (two and a half years ago) I found that he was being widely talked of for the Presidency of the Congress at its approaching yearly meeting.

Conspicuous in Indian educational work and a founder of the large and flourishing Anglo-Vedic College in Lahore, he has for a dozen years or more held the position of either Vice-President or Honourary Secretary of the College, and also that of Lecturer in History.

He started *The Punjabee,* a leading paper in the province, published in English, and has edited a monthly magazine and a weekly paper printed in the vernacular, besides writing for other Indian periodicals and for reviews in London.

The Arya Samaj, an important, fast growing and

influential movement of religious reform in India, which rejects idolatry and caste and is active in promoting education, social reforms and the elevation of woman, counts Mr. Rai among its honoured leaders.

He has organized relief work during periods of famine in India, and has for some years led in an extensive movement for the elevation of the "Depressed Classes," that is, the forty millions of "outcasts" or "untouchables" whose condition is so miserable. Several years ago I attended a National Conference to promote this work, at which he presided and delivered a powerful address.

Mr. Lajpat Rai has made three or four extended visits to England and three to America. In England he has spoken in many cities as a delegate from the National Indian Congress, for the purpose of acquainting the British public with the real condition of things in India, and to urge upon the British Government the granting to the Indian people of certain important political reforms. In America he has made a careful study of our history and institutions, our industrial and social movements, our political and religious life, and especially our schools and universities, and our educational systems and methods. He is impressed with the leadership which the United States is attaining in the world of education, particularly education in scientific, industrial, technological and agricultural directions, and he finds much here which he desires to see introduced into his own country.

From the beginning of the New National Movement in India, Mr. Rai has been one of its most prominent leaders. He is an ardent patriot, is proud of his country, her civilization, her literature and her great place in the world's history, and he believes she is destined to have a great future, commensurate with her great past. But now she is a subject land, ruled by a foreign power, her own people having practically no voice in the direction of their own national affairs or the shaping of their future destiny. This deeply grieves and galls him, as it does a large part of the Indian people. The Nationalist Movement, of which he gives an account in this book, is a protest against present political conditions, and a demand for larger freedom and independence. Indeed, its aim is self-rule; not necessarily severance of connection with the British Empire, but partnership in the Empire,—home rule inside the Empire like that enjoyed by Canada, Australia and South Africa.

The British Government of India frowns upon this Nationalist Movement, tries to suppress it, and places its leaders under ban. This is the way despotic governments always treat subject peoples as soon as they grow restive in their bonds and try to loosen them or throw them off. Mr. Lajpat Rai has had to pay heavily for his patriotism. In 1907 he was seized by the Government and, without trial or even being told what was his offence, was secretly sent away to prison in Burmah, and kept there six months. He was suspected of disloyalty and sedition, but not the slightest evidence was found against him. His only crime was that he was a Nationalist, and was working in perfectly open and legal ways to secure greater liberty for his country. After his release from prison, he brought legal suits against two newspapers, one in India and one in London, that had published charges of sedition against him; and, notwithstanding the fact that the powerful influence of the Government was on the side of the papers, he won both suits,— so clear was his case.

For a full dozen years India has been seething with unrest, seething with dissatisfaction over present political conditions. During the past ten years there has been not a little bomb throwing and not a few signs of revolution. When the present European war broke out there were at once increased outward expressions of loyalty; but the unrest has remained. When the war is over what will happen? That will depend, Mr. Lajpat Rai believes, upon the course pursued by the British Government. If the Government in a generous spirit meets India's just demands, there will be no revolution. If the Government blindly and obstinately refuses, the worst may happen.

While Mr. Rai is an ardent and uncompromising advocate of the Nationalist Cause, he has always counselled procedure by evolutionary and not by revolutionary measures, by vigorous and determined agitation and not by bomb throwing. Throughout his entire career he has striven by every means, through speech and the press, in India and in England, to move the British Government to prevent revolution, in what he believes is the only possible way, namely, by inaugurating and carrying out honestly a policy of justice to the Indian people.

There is in sight an Indian *Renaissance*. There is a "New India in the Making." Indeed the stirrings of new life in India are hardly less marked, less profound or less revolutionary, than in Japan or China. Of this the book gives a vivid and reliable picture,—and, what is of great importance, a picture from the inside.

We have many books which portray Indian conditions as foreigners see them,—particularly as they are seen by Christian missionaries and by the British rulers of the country. At last we have a book which gives us the life, the experiences, the wrongs, the sufferings, the hopes, the aims, the motives, and, what at the present time is most important of all, the political ideals and ambitions of the Indian people themselves, portrayed by one of their own number, a leader who has been in the very heart of the struggle from the beginning, and who has felt it all in his own life and his own soul.

It is a message to every man and woman in America, and in Great Britain, too, who loves justice and hates oppression, and who wants to know about one of the most heroic struggles for liberty now going on in the world.

My own intimate acquaintance with India for many years gives me a greatly increased sense of the value of Mr. Rai's book. Perhaps nothing in the volume will be found more surprising or more interesting to Americans than the overwhelming evidence of the dissatisfaction of India with her present political condition, and the fact that the Indian people want home rule, want it more earnestly than they want anything else, and that probably nothing less than this will keep them loyal to Great Britain. This feeling, which had been growing fast for years before the war broke out, has since sprung into a passion. And we may be sure that the flame will not burn with less intensity when the soldiers return who have been risking their lives for Great Britain in Turkey and Egypt and France, and who have been learning new lessons of self-reliance, freedom and independence from their contact with the great world.

It is hardly possible today to take up an Indian periodical of any kind, Hindu or Mohammedan, secular or religious (I myself regularly subscribe for and read nine, two of the number making a specialty of a monthly summary of Indian press opinion), without being brought upon some expression of this universal desire for self-rule. The people are disposed to be patient and considerate, and make no demands upon the Government that will be embarrassing so long as the war lasts. But everything indicates that when peace comes they will be in no mood to be treated like children and put off with the usual vague and meaningless promises.

Since India has borne faithfully and loyally her part in the war, one of the distinct stipulations in the treaty of peace at the end should be the granting to her of home rule. This is as much her right as is autonomy the right of Belgium or Poland. This right is recognized by not a few Englishmen; it should be recognized by the whole nation, and put into effect generously, freely, without waiting for struggle and bloodshed. The advantage to Great Britain would be incalculable. It would remove from her as a nation her most threatening danger, and it would give to her Empire a solidity and permanent strength such as it cannot otherwise secure.

While India wants freedom to shape her own affairs, her wisest minds do not desire separation from England. They recognize many strong ties between the two countries which they would not see broken. While they are determined not much longer to lie prostrate beneath England's feet, they would gladly stand by her side, arm in arm with her, firmly united for great ends of mutual welfare and mutual strength. An Anglo-Indian Empire is one of the splendid possibilities of the future, binding Britain and her colonies and her great Asiatic possession together into a powerful world-spanning federation of free peoples. Something like this is the dream of India's greatest leaders, as it is also the dream of not a few of Britain's most far-seeing minds.

When this world-revolutionizing war is over, Great Britain must reshape after a larger and more adequate pattern her whole scheme of Imperial Government. She must become a Federated Empire. There must be self-government at home, not only for Ireland but also for Scotland, Wales and England. And there must be self-government abroad, not only for Canada, Australasia and South Africa, but, as not less imperative and not less wise, for India also, to be followed in time, as conditions can be made favourable, by self-rule more or less complete for all of Britain's more important dependencies.

The danger is that Britain may forget India or thrust her aside, as in the past, to the position of a mere dependency. If she does this she will plant a cancer in the heart of her Empire, she will create a volcano under her throne. It will take courage and large statesmanship to give India home rule, as it took large statesmanship and courage to give home rule to South Africa. But the splendid venture must be made. And, made in the right spirit, it will succeed as perfectly as it did in South Africa.

Has Great Britain statesmen sufficiently far-sighted, with adequate genius and courage, to do to India the splendid justice of giving her the home rule which is her right, and then to create a world-circling federation of free peoples with India a partner in it,—a real Anglo-Indian Empire? It would be the most brilliant, constructive and noble work of statesmanship known to the modern world.

Now that Canadians, Australians, New Zealanders and South Africans as well as Englishmen, Scotchmen, Welshmen and Irishmen have fought side by side with the soldiers of India, shedding their blood in a common cause, why should they not all gladly welcome those heroic and loyal men of the East to a place by their side in the Empire which they have helped to save?

Need England shrink from the risk? This is her path of least risk. Under present conditions India is her peril. The one thing that will transform India from a source of ever-increasing danger to a bulwark of strength, is to trust her as South Africa has been trusted. She is certainly as worthy of trust as South Africa was. Thus to trust her, and to lift her up to a responsible place in the Empire, will appeal to India's pride as it has never been appealed to, will create in her an enthusiasm of loyalty equal to anything seen in any of the self-ruling colonies, will bind her to Great Britain with bands of steel.

Is it said that India is incapable of ruling herself? That was said of South Africa; that was said of Canada; that was said of the American Colonies when they broke off from Great Britain and set up a Government of their own; that is what England has long been saying of Ireland. That is what every nation that loves power always says of every section of its people that wants more liberty.

The truth is, the safest Government in the world for every people of any intellectual and moral development at all (and India is advanced, both intellectually and morally) is self-government. No rule so completely destroys the fibre of a nation as rule by a foreign power. India can rule herself far better than any foreign nation can rule her.

If India is incapable of self-government today, what an indictment is that against England! She was not thus incapable before England came. Has one hundred and fifty years of British tutelage produced such deterioration? India was possessed of a high civilization and of developed Governments long before England or any part of Central, Western or Northern Europe had emerged from barbarism. For three thousand years before England's arrival in the Orient, Indian Kingdoms and Empires had held leading places in Asia, and that means in the world. Some of the ablest rulers, statesmen, generals and financiers known to history, as well as many of the greatest thinkers and writers of mankind, have been of India's production. How is it, then, that she suddenly becomes imbecile and unable to stand on her own feet or conduct her own affairs as soon as England appears on the scene?

To be sure, at the time when England came, India was in a peculiarly disorganized and unsettled state; for it should be remembered that the Mogul Empire was just breaking up and new political adjustments were everywhere just being made,—a fact which accounts for England's being able to gain political power in India at all. But everything indicates that if India had not been interfered with by European nations, she would soon have been under competent Governments of her own again.

A further answer to the assertion that India cannot govern herself — surely one that should be conclusive — is the fact that, in parts, she is governing herself now, and governing herself well. It is notorious that the very best Government in India today is not that carried on by the British, but that of several of the Native States, notably Baroda and Mysore. In these States, particularly Baroda, the people are more free, more prosperous, more contented, and are making more progress, than in any other part of India. Note the superiority of both these States in the important matter of popular education. Mysore is spending on education more than three times as much per capita as is British India, while Baroda has made her education free and compulsory. Both of these States, but especially Baroda, which has thus placed herself in line with the leading nations of Europe and America by making provisions for the education of all her children, may well be contrasted with British India, which provides education, even of the poorest kind, for only one boy in ten and one girl in one hundred and forty-four.

The only ground at all that exists for the claim that the Indian people are not able to govern themselves lies in the fact that the British Government during all its history in the land has deprived them, and still continues to deprive them, against their constant protest, of practical experience in Government management. They had such experience before the British came, but since that time they have been robbed of it to their great injury. Of course, under present conditions, if the British should leave India in a day, with no body of men trained to take their places, for a time there would be confusion, just as there would be confusion in England if everybody there accustomed to Government management should leave that country in a day.

But the Indian people do not ask England to leave India in a day, or to leave at all; what they ask is for England to associate with herself the competent men of India in the government of their own country, and thus give them the experience in self-rule which is their right and of which they never ought to have been deprived. With such opportunities for practical experience extended to them for twenty years, or even for ten years, they would be ready for the full responsibilities of home rule.

Among the tens of thousands of India's educated men, and men of natural capacity for leadership, there is no lack of material to fill, and fill well as soon as they are given experience, every kind of official position. Many of the highest judgeships are now filled with great efficiency by Indians. In no department of the Government where Indians have been adequately tried have they been found wanting.

The truth is, not one single fact can be cited to show that India cannot govern herself well if given a chance. It would not be difficult to form an Indian Parliament today, composed of men as able and of as high character as those that constitute the fine Parliament of Japan. India has public men who, if they lived in England and belonged to the English race, would unhesitatingly be adjudged not only of Parliamentary but of Cabinet rank. For twenty years before his recent lamented death Mr. Gokhale was confessedly the equal in intellectual ability and in moral worth of any Englishman in India, not excepting the three Viceroys under whom he served. It is no exaggeration to declare that Mr. Justice Renade had qualifications fully fitting him for the position of Viceroy, or if he had lived in England, fitting him for the position of Premier.

This is only another way of saying that among the leaders of the various States and Provinces of

India there is abundant material to form National and Provincial Governments little, if at all, inferior in ability and in moral character to the Governments of the Western world.

J. T. SUNDERLAND.

New York, June, 1916.

CONTENTS

ILLUSTRATIONS

PREFACE TO THE SECOND EDITION

Considering that in August, 1916, when this book was published, I was only a stranger in this country, known only to a few individuals, with almost no credentials of any kind to command the attention of the reading public, it is extremely gratifying that the first edition should have been sold out in less than six months. The fact can only be explained by the broad-minded sympathy of the American public for the "under dog." I had a story to tell which the American public decided was worthy of being heard. So they heard it and now that they have heard it they want more of it.

In launching a second edition I take the opportunity of thanking the American press for their most generous and kindly appreciation of my little work. To the London Liberal press represented by the *Nation* and the *New Statesman* also I pay my acknowledgments. Their kindly reception shows the genuineness of their liberalism which, by the by, is the most valuable asset of English public life. Compare with this the treatment that has been accorded to me and my book by the British Indian Government. The first thing they did to injure me was to get the High Court at Lahore to cancel my license as a lawyer in the Punjab, India, on the ground of my being the author of a pamphlet called "Some Reflections on the Political Situation in

India," to which they objected and which they barred from entry into British India. This order is of course illegal; but the High Court of the Punjab has not a high reputation for its legal attainments and is always a willing instrument of the Executive. Then came the order barring this book. This by itself ought to be sufficient to show off the amount of political freedom we enjoy in India, but the year 1916 has been made memorable in the political history of India by other events of even a more significant character. Throughout the year, the Government in India continued to prosecute an English lady of world-wide fame, for the simple reason that that lady had the audacity of identifying herself with the "Home Rule of India" movement. Mrs. Annie Besant is an English woman of international fame. She is one of the most accomplished and eloquent platform speakers which the English speaking nations possess. She is a distinguished author and the revered head of the Theosophical Society which has ramifications all over the world. In addition to her religious and social and literary activities Mrs. Annie Besant has for some years been taking an active interest in the Indian Nationalist movement. She owns and edits two papers, one a daily and the other a weekly, both written in English and published at Madras, India, in the interests of Indian Nationalism. She is the founder and President of an Indian Home Rule League. She is an outspoken critic of the Russian methods of repression, suppression and confiscation that are in vogue in the Indian Administration. During Lord Hardinge's viceroyalty her criticism was tolerated, as the Head of the Government was known to be friendly to her. As soon, however, as Lord Hardinge turned his back on India, Mrs. Besant's good luck abandoned her and down came the hand of the Madras Government. The first order against her demanded security for her daily paper, *New India.* This security was duly furnished and has since been confiscated and a new security of a much larger sum has been demanded. Mrs. Besant has complied with these orders also, though under protest and is contesting them in the courts. One court has rejected her appeal, holding that though the order of the Government was illegal, the statutes gave them no power to give relief. She is now appealing to the Judicial Committee of the Privy Council, in London, and the matter rests there. Two other Provincial Governments, those of Bombay and the Central Provinces, took action to restrict her liberty of movement, by prohibiting her entry into their respective jurisdictions, under the Defence of India Act. All this has made a sensation and Mrs. Annie Besant is one of the most popular persons in India at the present moment. She is considered a heroine and the Nationalist party is backing her up fully. Her financial losses have been made up to her and her papers are flourishing Her Home Rule League is spreading.

Mrs. Annie Besant has not, however, been the only recipient of Government attention during the course of the year. The Nationalist leader, Bal Ganga Dhar Tilak, has been persecuted in various ways. A Magistrate was found to adjudge some of his speeches in favour of Home Rule as seditious and on the basis of that adjudication, Mr. Tilak was ordered to deposit security of over $13,000 for good behaviour for a year, the object being to gag him. On Mr. Tilak appealing to the High Court the Judges quashed the order, holding that the speeches, read as a whole, did not violate the law. He is, however, still being followed and persecuted otherwise.

Press Act. The following resolution passed by the Council of the Bombay Presidency Association in connection with the proceedings taken by the Government against Mrs. Besant's *New India* speaks for itself:

"Having regard to the arbitrary character of the provisions of the Press Act of 1910 and the manner in which it has been enforced in the case of several newspapers, and recently in the case of *New India,* thereby causing public dissatisfaction and discontent, this Council is of opinion that a representation should be submitted to the Government by the Association pointing out the oppressive character of the Act and its administration and asking for its appeal. The Council, therefore, resolves, that a committee consisting of Sir Narayan Chandavarkar, Messrs. B. G. Horniman, D. N. Bahadurji, A. M. Jinnah and the Honorary Secretaries be appointed to draft a memorial for the purpose and submit it to the Council within a fortnight."

Political Crime in Bengal. In Bengal there has been no falling off in the activities of the Revolutionary party in spite of the fact that the powers taken by the Government under the Defence of India Act have been ruthlessly exercised. The following extracts taken from a press comment on the Resolution of the Government of Bengal relating to the working of the Police Department in 1915 may be of some interest in this connection:

"The Resolution of the Bengal Government on the Report of the Police administration in the Presidency for 1915 says that the criminal record of the year was a black one. Serious crime of all kinds except rioting showed considerable increase, which was most marked in the case of offences against property. True cases of dacoity increased from 289 in 1914 to 643 in 1915, burglary cases from 30,294 to 39,812 and theft cases from 17,730 to 31,552. The increase in theft and burglary may be ascribed mainly to the unfavourable economic conditions caused by partial crop failures in many districts of the province and by a heavy fall in the price of jute. In the case of dacoity, however, there appears to be good reason for attributing the increase almost entirely to the state of unrest caused by the war.

"Referring to revolutionary crime in Bengal the resolution says: The outbreak of revolutionary crime in the early part of the year was followed by a lull after the introduction of the Defence of India Act in April. The latter part of the year was, however, marked by renewed activity on the part of the revolutionary party and the total number of cases believed to be connected with the movement was 36 as compared with 12 in the previous year. These cases included 34 dacoities, 2 attempted dacoities, 9 murders and one attempted bomb outrage.

"With regard to the circulation of seditious literature, the report of the Inspector General of Police says: Increased activity in the circulation of seditious leaflets came to notice about June and continued throughout the year. Under the existing law mere possession of seditious matter is not an offence and consequently there are no means of checking the serious evil at the fountain head. It is only after the seditious and inflammatory matter has been circulated and mischief done that the law can be put in motion. There is convincing evidence that the revolutionary party in Bengal depend largely upon seditious literature to recruit their ranks and several youths have confessed that they were drawn into the movement through reading leaflets issued by the revolutionists. Penalising the possession of seditious matter may not be a complete cure for the evil, but it will materially assist to check it."

As recently as December 11, 1916, the Governor laid renewed emphasis upon the continued existence of serious political crime in Bengal and of their failure to check or extirpate it.

Since then a new ordinance has been promulgated making the mere possession of seditious literature penal.

In the Punjab the Government prosecuted a third batch of persons on charges of political conspiracy, six of whom have since been sentenced to death and the others to varying terms of imprisonment and transportation.

The united demand for autonomy. The most significant political event of the year, however, is the presentation to the Viceroy of a joint memorandum of post-war reforms signed by nineteen out of twenty-two elected members of the Viceroy's Legislative Council. In the opinion of the signatories this is the minimum which will satisfy Indian public opinion *for the present*. The demands are not far-reaching enough on the way to autonomy but the document is remarkable as a symbol of unity between the different religious communities and castes of the Indian population, on the so-called lack of which the British Imperialist so much relies, in justification of denying self-government to India. Coming from men of varying shades of political opinion, pledged by their oath of allegiance to loyalty to the British Government and by their connection with the latter, the document is the most conclusive and scathing condemnation of the existing system of Government in India. We make no apology for giving the document in full.

MEMORANDUM submitted to H. E., the Viceroy, by the undersigned elected Additional Members of the Imperial Legislative Council with regard to Post-War reforms.

There is no doubt that the termination of the war will see a great advance in the ideals of government all over the civilised world and especially in the British Empire, which entered into the struggle in defence of the liberties of weak and small nationalities and is pouring forth its richest blood and treasure in upholding the cause of justice and humanity in the international relations of the world. India has borne her part in this struggle and cannot remain unaffected by the new spirit of change for a better state of things. Expectations have been raised in this country and hopes held out that, after the war, the problems of Indian Administration will be looked at from a new angle of vision. The people of India have good reasons to be grateful to England for the great progress in her material resources and the widening of her intellectual and political outlook under British rule, and for the steady, if slow, advance in her national life commencing with the Charter Act of India of 1833. Up to 1909, the Government of India was conducted by a bureaucracy almost entirely non-Indian in its composition and not responsible to the people of India. The reforms of 1909 for the first time introduced an Indian element in the direction of affairs in the administration of India. This element was of a very limited character. The Indian people accepted it as an indication on the part of the Government of a desire to admit the Indians into the inner counsels of the Indian Empire. So far as the Legislative Councils are concerned, the number of non-official members was merely enlarged with increased facilities for debate and interpellation. The Supreme Legislative Council retained an absolute official majority, and in the Provincial Legislative Councils, where a non-official majority was allowed, such majority included nominated members and the European representatives. In measures largely affecting the people, whether of legislation or taxation, by which Europeans were not directly affected, the European members would naturally support the Government, and the nominated members, being nominees of Government, would be inclined to take the same side. Past experience has shown that this has actually happened on various occasions. The non-official majorities, therefore, in the Provincial Councils have proved largely illusory and give no real power to the representatives of the people. The Legislative Councils, whether Supreme or Provincial, are at present nothing but advisory bodies without any power of effective control over the Government, Imperial or Provincial. The people or their representatives are practically as little associated with the real government of the country as they were before the reforms, except for the introduction of the Indian element in the Executive Councils, where again the nomination rests entirely with the Government, the people having no voice in the selection of the Indian members.

The object which the Government had in view in introducing the reforms of 1909 was, as expressed by the Prime Minister in his speech in the House of Commons on the second reading of the Indian Councils Bill (1st April, 1909), that "it was most desirable in the circumstances to give to the people of India the feeling that these Legislative Councils are not mere automatons the wires of which are pulled by the official hierarchy." This object, it is submitted, has not been attained. Apart from this question of the Constitution of the Legislative and Executive Councils, the people labour under certain grave disabilities, which not only prevent the utilisation, but also lead to the wastage, of what is best in them, and are positively derogatory to their sense of national self-respect. The Arms Act which excludes from its operation Europeans and Anglo-Indians and applies only to the pure natives of the country, the disqualification of Indians for forming or joining Volunteer corps, and their exclusion from the commissioned ranks of the Army, are disabilities which are looked upon with an irritating sense of racial differentiation. It would be bad enough if these were mere disabilities. Restrictions and prohibitions regarding the possession and use of arms have tended to emasculate the civil populations in India and expose them to serious danger. The position of Indians in India is practically this, that they have no real part or share in the direction of the government of the country, and are placed under very great and galling disabilities from which the other members of the British Empire are exempt and which have reduced them to a state of utter helplessness. The existence, moreover, of the system of indentured emigration gives to the British Colonies and the outside world the impression that Indians, as a whole, are no better than indentured coolies, who are looked upon as very little, if at all, above the slave. The present state of things makes the Indians feel that, though theoretically they are equal subjects of the King, they hold a very inferior position in the British Empire. Other Asiatic races also hold the same, if not a worse, view about India and her status in the Empire. Humiliating as this position of inferiority is to the Indian mind, it is almost unbearable to the youth of India whose outlook is broadened by education and travel in foreign parts where they come in contact with other free races.

In the face of these grievances and disabilities, what has sustained the people is the hope and faith inspired by promises and assurances of fair and equal treatment which have been held out from time to time by our Sovereigns and British statesmen of high standing. In the crisis we are now going through, the Indian people have sunk domestic differences between themselves and the Government and have faithfully and loyally stood by the Empire. The Indian soldiers were eager to go to the battlefields of Europe, not as mercenary troops but as free citizens of the British Empire which required their services, and her civilian population was animated by one desire, namely, to stand by England in the hour of her need. Peace and tranquillity reigned throughout India when she was practically denuded of British and Indian troops. The Prime Minister of England, while voicing the sentiments of the English people in regard to India's part in this great war, spoke of Indians as "the joint and equal custodians of one common interest and future." India does not claim any reward for her loyalty, but she has a right to expect that the want of confidence on the part of the Government, to which she not unnaturally ascribes her present state, should now be a thing of the past and that she should no longer occupy a position of subordination but one of comradeship. This would assure the Indian people that England is ready and willing to help them to attain self-government under the ægis of the British Crown, and thus discharge the noble mission which she has undertaken and to which she has so often given voluntary expression through her rulers and statesmen. What is wanted is not merely good government or efficient administration, but government that is acceptable to the people because it is responsible to them. This is what India understands would constitute the changed angle of vision.

If, after the termination of the war, the position of India practically remains what it was before, and there is no material change in it, it will undoubtedly cause bitter disappointment and great discontent in the country, and the beneficent effects of participation in common danger, overcome by common effort will soon disappear, leaving no record behind save the painful memory of unrealised expectations. We feel sure that the Government is also alive to the situation and is contemplating measures of reform in the administration of the country. We feel that we should avail ourselves of this opportunity to respectfully offer to Government our humble suggestions as to the lines on which reforms should proceed. They must, in our opinion, go to the root of the matter. They must give to the people real and effective participation in the government of the country, and also remove those irritating disabilities as regards the possession of arms and a military career, which indicate want of confidence in the people and place them in a position of inferiority and helplessness. With this view, we would take the liberty to suggest the following measures for consideration and adoption:

1. In all the Executive Councils, Provincial and Imperial, half the number of members should be Indians; the European element in the Executive Councils should, as far as possible, be nominated from the ranks of men trained and educated in the public life of England, so that India may have the benefit of a wider outlook and larger experience of the outside world. It is not absolutely essential that the members of the Executive Councils, Indians or Europeans, should have experience of actual administration, for, as in the case of Ministers in England, the assistance of the permanent officials of the departments is always available to them. As regards Indians, we venture to say that a sufficient number of qualified Indians, who can worthily fill the office of members of the Executive Council and hold portfolios, is always available. Our short experience in this direction has shown how Indians like Sir S. P. Sinha, Sir Syed Ali Imam, the late Mr. Krishnaswami Iyer, Sir Shams-ul-Huda and Sir Sankaran Nair have maintained a high level of administrative ability in the discharge of their duties. Moreover, it is well known that the Native States,

where Indians have opportunities, have produced renowned administrators like Sir Salar Jang, Sir T. Madhava Rao, Sir Sheshadri Ayer, Dewan Bahadur Raghuṇath Rao, not to mention the present administrators in the various Native States of India. The statutory obligation, now existing, that three of the members of the Supreme Executive Council shall be selected from the public services in India and similar provisions with regard to Provincial Councils should be removed. The elected representatives of the people should have a voice in the selection of the Indian members of the Executive Councils and for that purpose a principle of election should be adopted.

2. All the Legislative Councils in India should have a substantial majority of elected representatives. These representatives, we feel sure, will watch and safeguard the interests of the masses and the agricultural population, with whom they are in closer touch than any European officer, however sympathetic, can possibly be. The proceedings of the various Legislative Councils and the Indian National Congress and the Moslem League bear ample testimony to the solicitude of the educated Indians for the welfare of the masses and their acquaintance with their wants and wishes. The franchise should be broadened and extended directly to the people, Mohammedans or Hindus, wherever they are in a minority, being given proper and adequate representation, having regard to their numerical strength and position.

3. The total number of the members of the Supreme Council should be not less than 150, and of the Provincial Councils not less than 100 for the major provinces, and not less than 60 to 75 for the minor provinces.

4. The Budget should be passed in the shape of

money bills, fiscal autonomy being conceded to India.

5. The Imperial Legislative Council should have power to legislate on, and discuss and pass resolutions relating to, all matters of Indian administration, and the Provincial Councils should have similar powers with regard to Provincial administrations, save and except that the direction of military affairs, of foreign relations, declarations of war, the making of peace, and the entering into treaties, other than commercial, should be vested in the Government of India. As a safeguard, the Governor-General-in-Council or the Governor-in-Council, as the case may be, should have the right of veto, which, however, should be exercised subject to certain conditions and limitations.

6. The Council of the Secretary of State should be abolished. The Secretary of State should, as far as possible, hold in relation to the Government of India a position similar to that which the Secretary of State for the Colonies holds in relation to the Colonies. The Secretary of State should be assisted by two permanent Under-Secretaries, one of whom should be an Indian. The salaries of the Secretary and the Under-Secretaries should be placed on the British estimates.

7. In any scheme of Imperial Federation, India should be given through her chosen representatives a place similar to that of the self-governing dominions.

8. The Provincial Governments should be made autonomous, as stated in the Government of India's despatch dated 25th August, 1911.

9. The United Provinces, as well as the other major provinces should have a Governor brought from the United Kingdom and should have an Executive Council.

10. A full measure of local self-government should be immediately granted.

11. The right to carry arms should be granted to Indians on the same conditions as to Europeans.

12. Indians should be allowed to enlist as volunteers and units of a territorial army established in India.

13. Commissions in the Army should be given to Indian youths under conditions similar to those applicable to Europeans.

MANINDRA CHANDRA NANDY OF KASIMBAZAR.
D. E. WACHA.
BHUPENDRANATH BASU.
BISHAN DUTT SHUKUL.
MADAN MOHAN MALAVIYA.
K. V. RANGASWAMIENGAR.
MAZHARUL HAQUE.
V. S. SRINIVASAN.
TEJ BAHADUR SAPRU.
IBRAHIM RAHIMTOOLA.
B. NARASIMHESWARA SARMA.
MIR ASAD ALI.
KAMINI KUMAR CHANDA.
KRISHNA SAHAY.
R. N. BHANJA DEO OF KANIKA.
M. B. DADABHOY.
SITA NATH ROY.
MOHAMED ALI MOHAMED.
M. A. JINNAH.

It might be noted that the demands are extremely moderate and accompanied by rather exaggerated acknowledgments of the effects of British rule in India. They proceed from a body of professed loyalists. They have received wide support from representative organisations of Hindus and Mahommedans as well as from representative men of all classes, castes and denominations.

India in England. In England the exigencies of the war have left no time for the British Parliament to devote to the meagre discussions of Indian affairs that followed the presentation of East India accounts once a year. The requirements of the law in this respect have been conveniently ignored. In the press too, while every expression of loyalty is lauded to the skies and even cabled to America, the demands for rights and reforms are silently ignored or hooted with contempt. The reactionary Lord Sydenham has, however, sounded a note of alarm urging the "immediate and final" rejection of the demands made by the nineteen members of the Viceroy's Legislative Council. The London *Nation* and the *New Statesman* have come out with sympathetic articles.

India in America. Here in the United States of America the attention paid to Indian affairs by the American press, has elicited long statements by British statesmen in connection with their rule in India. The Secretary of State for India, the Under Secretary of State for India, the Viceroy, the Lieutenant Governor of the Punjab, the Finance Minister have all granted interviews to American correspondents, assuring the latter of the marvellous progress India is making under British rule, of the prosperity and loyalty of India and of the extreme unimportance of the Nationalist party. Judged from these interviews India must be a very paradise on earth — a garden of Eden. Most of the statements are vague and misleading, containing half truths and suppressing important facts. I will pick up one statement for purposes of illustration. The Finance Minister of India is reported to have said:

"So far from the people of India groaning under an enormous burden of taxation India is one of the most lightly taxed countries on the face of the earth. . . . The total Revenue, Imperial and Provincial, for the current year amounted to £86,500,000 and this sum distributed among the 244,000,000 people of British India gave a resultant contribution per capita of only seven shillings."

Now at best this is only a half truth. The Finance Minister should have added that the total income of India is about £600,000,000 a year, bringing the average per capita to £2 a year. Seven shillings out of £2 a year is perhaps the heaviest tax paid by any country on the face of the earth. Equally misleading are other statements about land tax, etc., which I am noticing in my new book dealing with Economic Effects of British Rule in India which is going to the press soon.

The writer is also establishing a kind of Bureau in New York, where all kinds of information, political, economic, legal, commercial, etc., relating to India will be supplied to the American public.

LAJPAT RAI.

New York,
19th January, 1917.

P. S. Since the above was written the newspapers have reported that the British Government have decided to raise a war loan of $500,000,000 in India as a "free gift" to Great Britain. Free gift, indeed! Where the donor and the donee are the same—a free gift by a people vast numbers of whom do not get two meals a day and have an average income of ten dollars a year. Imperialism, wonderful are thy feats!!!

NOTE: The *Manchester Guardian*, March 13, 1917, comments as follows upon the war loan mentioned in the above P. S., the italics being mine:

"Why was this question of a financial contribution from India raised now? *For our own part we have the gravest doubt as to the wisdom or justice of taking any financial contribution from India.* We believe that this is not the best way for India and for the Empire, in which India can serve the common cause, and *that the loss it represents to an extremely poor population like that of India is very much greater than the gain it represents to England.* If we really are seriously concerned that India 'should develop in every way the vast potentialities of her indigenous products' it would be better to spend 100 millions [£] on developing her resources than to take that money from India and in exchange give Bombay a tariff."

LAJPAT RAI.

18th March, 1917.

INTRODUCTION

I

DURING my travels in the world, the one point that has struck me most forcibly and most painfully, is the lack of true knowledge about the affairs of India among the "civilised" nations of the globe. Even the best educated among them know very little about India and what little they know is not always right. The sources from which the ordinary stay-at-home Westerner derives his knowledge about India are the following: (a) missionaries who have been to India, (b) English writers of the class of Rudyard Kipling and Sir Valentine Chirol, (c) British officials, (d) serious students of Indian history or Indian literature like the late Professor Max Müller, the late Miss Noble, and the late Professor Goldstucker.

Now unfortunately for India most of these people, except those coming under the last heading, have generally an axe to grind and can not be accepted as disinterested, well-informed, impartial authorities. Their reading of Indian history is often perverted and their observations of Indian life partial and distorted. They go to India with definite aims, look at persons and things from their own particular angle, and pose as authorities on matters far beyond the scope of their observations and studies. With rare exceptions most of the Westerners who go to India go with the presumption that the people of India belong to an inferior level of society; that they are heathens, worshippers of stocks and stones; that they are hopelessly divided into castes and classes; that these castes and classes are always at each other's throats; that they have never had a settled or civilised form of government; that the British have for the first time in their history given them a settled government; and that India would go to pieces if British government were to withdraw.

Writers about India may again be broadly subdivided into two classes: (a) those of British origin, (b) those of non-British origin. Those of British origin are in ninety-nine cases out of a hundred tainted with the imperial bias. They can only look at things from the imperial or British point of view. Even the best and the most fair-minded of them do not altogether succeed in freeing themselves from this bias. The bias acts even against their will. The second class of writers are affected by the racial and the colour bias. Moreover, nine out of ten amongst them are made to look at things from the British point of view. As soon as they land at an Indian port, they are taken in hand by the British residents, officials and non-officials, and practically the whole of their trip is arranged for them by the latter. They only see things which the ruling community want them to see and they only hear and know what these allow them to hear or know. The few who resolutely refuse to be thus "programmed" do sometimes see things in their true light, as the late Mr. Keir Hardie, M.P., and Mr. H. W. Nevinson did.

In this connection I think the following remarks of the latest American writer on India, Professor Pratt of Williams College, Massachusetts, in his book on "India and Its Faiths" are very pertinent. Professor Pratt begins by warning the reader against "the point of view of the native" himself, as well as against "those European writers who seek to give an ultra 'sympathetic' picture of India." But his observations about the other two of the four sources of information mentioned by him are extremely interesting. He says:

"Much greater is the danger that we, with our Western ideals and customs so different from those of India, should go to the other extreme and take one of the two remaining points of view that I referred to above. One of these is that which characterises a certain type (now happily decreasing) of earnest but narrow-minded missionary." The fourth source of information, which, according to Professor Pratt, "one should regard with distrust," comprises "the superficial tourist or the non-missionary European resident in India." In his opinion this source is particularly dangerous, for "it is so natural to suppose that one of our own race who has travelled in India (and especially one who has lived there 'twenty-two years') will be in a position to know all about it. . . . The tourist's ignorance is not surprising, but it is not easy to understand the ignorance of the average European resident in India." Professor Pratt's remarks about the "average European resident," who has been "twenty-two years" in India, are prefaced by an eulogistic tribute to the British administration of justice in India, which may be accepted with a little salt. The administration of justice in India is impartial and as fair as it can be under the circumstances, except when one party is a native and the other a Britisher. What concerns us here, is Professor Pratt's opinion about the resident Englishman's knowledge of India. In his opinion "most of the Englishmen" whom he met seemed to him "singularly lacking in curiosity or interest" about "Indian thought, religion, traditions and ways of viewing things." "The Anglo-Indian," adds he, "is surprisingly indifferent towards almost everything native." Professor Pratt illustrates his conclusions by actual facts which came under his observation. One English gentleman who had lived in Calcutta and other parts of the East for many years, said to the professor: "The natives are all just a lot of animals, don't you think so?" No wonder that the professor had to say that his impression was quite different. For him it was hard to conceive how one "could stay any time among them without finding them a truly lovable people, and without imbibing genuine respect and admiration for the simple dignity of their lives, the quiet courtesy of their manners, their uncomplaining endurance of hardships, their unbounded hospitality, and the feeling for spiritual value, which in spite of gross superstitions is unmistakable in the Indian atmosphere." Professor Pratt's "Englishman" had never heard of a Dr. Bose, "one of the greatest botanists living," and he did "not think much" of Tagore's poetry. "This lack of interest in native life as such," continues Mr. Pratt, "and the proud manifestation of conscious superiority that goes with it, shows itself in the coarser natures *in a contempt for the 'black man'* and 'a constant swagger of putting him in his place.' As a result of this indifference to and *contempt for the natives,* most of the Anglo-Indians that I know anything about are very ignorant concerning the religions of India, and *decidedly prejudiced against them.* Personally I think that the opinions of nine Englishmen out of ten on the subject of Indian religions are *entirely untrustworthy.*"[1]

Professor Pratt only speaks of the English residents' ignorance of Indian religion, but I am disposed to add that the opinions of ninety-nine out of every hundred Anglo-Indians on the nature and effects of British rule in India and the capacity of Indians to manage their own affairs are equally "*untrustworthy.*" Hence the colossal ignorance which prevails in the West about what is happening in India politically and economically. Just think of an honest, fair-minded British writer, like Lowes Dickinson, presuming to write about political life in India without discussing the economic effects of British rule.

India being only a dependency, her affairs do not attract that attention which they would if she were

[1] The italics everywhere in this quotation are mine.

a self-governing country. The British Parliament disposes of the Indian affairs by an annual discussion of a few hours in an extremely thin house. The last time the British House of Commons discussed an important measure affecting India, viz.: one by which it was proposed to suspend the Indian Civil Service examination pending the war and to authorise the Secretary of State in Council to make appointments by nomination, the maximum attendance, it is said, never exceeded 28. This measure was condemned by the unanimous voice of the Indian native press, yet there was nobody in the House to give expression to their views in the matter. The author, himself, has attended the sittings of the House in different years, when the India budget was under *discussion* and can testify from personal knowledge that the attendance was *always* very scanty and the speeches, often, poor.

Yet the fact that India is inhabited by about one-fifth of the whole human race and that her trading capacity is simply unlimited, entitles her to a fuller consideration at the hands of the civilised world. Leaving aside her past, it can not be doubted that she is destined to play a great part in the development of the near future. As such, the writer has presumed that the following brief account of the rise and development of the Indian Nationalist Movement may not be devoid of interest to British and American readers. The book is of course open to the objection that it is written by a "native," but in the eyes of impartial investigators that should be its merit. The writer has been closely associated with the movement for the last thirty-three years of his life, in almost all its phases, religious, social, educational, industrial and political. It was in 1888 that he joined the Indian National Congress, the official organisation of the "constitutional" nationalists, i.e., only four years after it was started.

In the following pages he has tried to give as faithful an account of the origin and progress of the movement as is possible under the circumstances. The one fact which qualifies him to interpret the Indian Nationalist Movement is that his position has always been more or less detached. He has generally had the confidence of all sections as far as the broad outlines of their policy were concerned, without identifying himself with each and every item of their respective programmes. Whenever occasionally or incidentally he has happened to know of any projected violence, without exception he has used his influence toward restraint. By a timely exercise of his influence he once (1908) succeeded in saving the lives of one Lieutenant Governor and one College Principal. The conduct of the British in India and their denial of the fundamental rights of the people, however, continue to add fuel to the fire and make it impossible for the friends of the constitutional movement to stop or effectually check the employment of physical force. Personally the writer is disposed to agree with the Lieutenant Governor of the Punjab, who said the other day, that open rebellion was morally less heinous than a campaign of underhand violence by bombs and revolvers; but what the Lieutenant Governor forgot to notice was that open rebellion by a subject people must always, in the nature of things, be preceded by secret propaganda and secret preparations. Secret preparations in a country like India, access to which is on all sides controlled by the British, are bound to bring in the use of explosives and the taking of measures which might paralyse the administration and weaken its hold on the people. If a Government muzzles its people, shuts out all open avenues of political propaganda, denies them the use of firearms and otherwise stands in the way of a free agitation for political changes, it is doubtful if it can reasonably complain of secret plots and secret propaganda as distinguished from open rebellion.

The American press has of late been giving out different versions of the political situation in India. One version affirms that India is on the point of rebellion; the other that India is devotedly loyal. Both statements are partially true and both are partially false. India is not devotedly loyal, yet to all appearances she is so. Nor is India on the verge of rebellion, though she is full of rebellious spirit. It is preposterous to contend that her expressions of loyalty on the outbreak of the war are proof that she is satisfied with British rule as it is. The anti-British movement is spreading and gaining strength every day, and it is impossible for the British Government without the aid of the Indian people to uproot what the British are pleased to characterise as "Anarchism."

II

Among other criticisms, to which this book may be subjected, I anticipate one or two on historical grounds which I would like to answer beforehand. It may be said that I have painted the early history of India as "a golden age"; that my references to Chandra Gupta and Asoka show only the bright side of the shield and that I have throughout assumed that India is, and has always been, a political unity. Now in considering this criticism, it should be borne in mind that my sole object in referring to the past history of India is to show to my reader that India was not a barbarous country when the British obtained possession of her, that she has had a long and in some respects a glorious history; that she was never before governed by foreigners from without in the political and economic interests of a nation not living within her territorial limits, as she has been and is being governed under the British. Whatever may be my personal opinions about ancient India and her civilisation, I have sufficient knowledge of the Occident to understand that the Western reader is liable to have some hesitancy about accepting them in all cases as historical truths. I have therefore carefully avoided making any statements for which I can not cite good authority. The statements made may be roughly divided into three kinds: (1) those relating to pre-Buddhist India, (2) those relating to India of 500 B. C. to about 1000 A. D., (3) those relating to India of Mohammedan domination.

Now, as regards the first, we have no strictly historical data and the statements are based on the contents of the literature of the period, viz., the religious treatises, the law books of the Hindus, and the epics. There is enough in this mass of literature to justify the modest statements made in the first chapter of this book about that period of Indian history, and, if necessary, I would be able to quote good authority for every statement made by me. Coming to the next period, viz., from 500 B. C. to 1000 A. D., we have enough historical data in the writings of the Greeks, the Chinese and the Mohammedans to justify the general statements made. It may be that my statements about this period are not complete, but that is because I am not writing a history of the period. I am only making an incidental reference for the purposes of this volume. For these purposes it is not necessary to trace the origin of Chandra Gupta's rule, or to state his motives for instituting a department of commerce or a department of vital statistics. Chandra Gupta himself may have been a "villain," but there is ample historical data for an historian like Vincent Smith [2]— a retired Indian Civil Servant by no means partial to India [3]— to conclude that "the foregoing review of the civil and the military system of government during the reign of Chandra Gupta proves clearly that Northern India in the time of Alexander the

[2] See Vincent Smith's "Early History of India," third edition, p. 135.

[3] "Mr. Vincent Smith is always anxious to deprive India of the credit of all her achievements in art and literature." Indian Historical Studies by Prof. H. D. G. Rawlinson, p. 227.

Great had attained to a high degree of civilisation *which must have been the product of evolution continued through many centuries."* [4]

As for Asoka, Vincent Smith has discredited the stories of his having been guilty of excesses ascribed to his early career by other historians. In any case, all historians are unanimous about the excellence of his administration. "The lofty moral tone of these edicts" (*i. e.,* Asoka's edicts), says Rawlinson (page 27 of "Indian Historical Studies"), "indicates clearly enough that India in the third century B. C. was a highly civilised country; it must, indeed, have compared favourably with the rest of the world of the time; for Greece was sinking fast into a state of corrupt decadence, and Rome, in the throes of her struggle with Carthage, had scarcely yet emerged from barbarism." No Indian need make any higher claim than this for the India of the third century B. C. Finally, as about the political unity of India in the past, let it be noted that I do not claim that India was *always* united under one political authority or even under one political system. At the same time it is equally untrue that India was never a political unity. Most of the British writers are disposed to deny that there has been or is any kind of unity in India. This may be disposed of by the following quotation from Vincent Smith's "Early History of India" (page 5): "India, encircled as she is by seas and mountains, is indisputably a geographical unit, and, as such, is rightly designated by one name. Her type of

[4] The italics in the above quotation are mine.

civilisation, too, has many features which differentiate it from that of all other regions of the world, while they are common to the whole country, or rather sub-continent, in a degree sufficient to justify its treatment as a unity in the history of the social, religious and intellectual development of mankind."[5] He adds, however, that "the *complete* political unity of India under the control of a permanent power, wielding unquestioned authority, is a thing of yesterday, barely a century old. The most notable of her rulers in the olden time cherished the ambition of universal Indian dominion, and severally attained it in a greater or lesser degree; not one of them, however, attained it completely." The point admits of great controversy and anything like a proper discussion would add to the bulk of this book so much as would be out of proportion to its bearing on the main subject. Mr. Vincent Smith admits that Asoka's Empire included the whole of India proper except a tiny bit of the Southern peninsula lying between Nellore and Cape Comorin. (See map of Asoka's Empire in his history, between pages 162–163.) The exclusion of this bit is based not on any positive evidence that this part was not included within his empire, but on the absence of positive evidence to the contrary. It is as if men living two thousand years after our day should expect it to be proved to their satisfaction

[5] See also Mr. E. B. Havell's Ideals of Indian Art, pp. 11-12. Mr. Havell's conclusion is: "We may see if we have eyes to see, that all India is one in spirit, however diverse in race and in creed."

by positive documentary evidence that every bit of India was included in the British Empire under Queen Victoria. Again, the fact that Asoka's Empire did not include the Southernmost part of the Indian Peninsula was more than compensated by the inclusion of almost the whole of Afghanistan and Beluchistan and Nepal in his dominions. The territories comprising the kingdom of Nepal are not included in the British Empire, although they constitute a necessary part of India. Yet even Vincent Smith does not doubt that India is a political unity to-day.

Then again it is only very recently that he and other historians have found out the data for a history of the Gupta Empire from 320 to 455 A. D., about the extent of which he says:

"The dominions under the direct government of Samundra Gupta in the middle of the fourth century thus comprised all the populous and fertile countries of Northern India. . . . Beyond those wide limits the frontier kingdoms of Assam and the Gangetic delta as well as those on the southern slopes of the Himalayas and the free tribes of Malwa and Rajputana were attached to the Empire by bonds of subordinate alliance; while almost all the kingdoms of the South had been overrun by the Emperor's armies and compelled to acknowledge his irresistible might.

"Whatever may have been the exact degree of skill attained by Samundra Gupta in the practice of the arts which graced his scanty leisure, it is clear that he was endowed with no ordinary powers; and that he was in fact a man of genius, who may fairly claim the title of the Indian Napoleon.

"By a strange irony of fate this great king — warrior, poet, and musician — who conquered nearly all India, and whose alliances extended from the Oxus to Ceylon — was unknown even by name to the historians until the publication of this work.[6] His lost fame has been slowly recovered by the minute and laborious study of inscriptions and coins during the last eighty years."

It may be mentioned, in passing, that monarchs of the Samundra Gupta type, who may be compared easily with a Charlemagne, a Frederick or a Peter the Great, have flourished in India almost every second generation. Hindu folk-lore has known them as Vikramadityas (Suns of Power) and has invested their names with "the halo of Arthurian romance." And this was a time in the history of the world when Egypt and Babylon had already passed away, when China was in a state of "anarchy," when the Roman Empire was under the heels of the barbarians, and when the Saracenic Empire (Caliphate) had not yet come into existence. England, France and Germany were simply *non est*.

Now, the history of India before 1000 A. D. has not yet been completely constructed, and who knows but that by future researches some other Samundra Guptas may be discovered? But in any case, the point is not so very important. In that sense even now, India may not be called a complete political

[6] First Edition, Clarendon Press, Oxford, 1905.

unity. It was not so in 1830 A.D. Up till 1849 the Punjab was independent and so were the other provinces annexed by Lord Dalhousie. So Vincent Smith's claim, that it has been so since 1818 A.D.[7] is not well founded. What is more important for our purpose is the present and the future. It is claimed that under the British, India is a political unity though Nepal is still independent.

The critics of Indian aspirations are very unfair, when they compare the India of the seventeenth or the eighteenth or even of the nineteenth century with Great Britain, Germany, France and United States of the twentieth. They forget that the political nations known by these names are only the growth of yesterday. India is as big as the whole of Europe excluding Russia. Yet what was Europe before the nineteenth century? It was a big camp of warring nations and warring religions, engaged in exterminating and persecuting each other alternately. India was more or less a political unity when Great Britain was smarting under the heels of the Romans. It took the British over 1600 years to establish their present political unity. Compare the following account of "England under foreign rule" (1013–1204), given by Green in his "Short History of the English People," with the condition of things in India from the time of Samundra Gupta onwards.

"Britain had become England in the five hundred years that followed the landing of Hengest, and its

[7] See footnote to p. 5, of his "Early History of India," 3rd ed.

conquest had ended in the settlement of its conquerors. . . . But whatever titles kings might assume, or however imposing their rule might appear, Northumbrian remained apart from West Saxon, Dane from Englishman.

"Through the two hundred years that lie between the flight of Aethelred from England to Normandy and that of John from Normandy to England our story is a story of foreign rule. Kings from Denmark were succeeded by kings from Normandy, and these by kings from Anjou. Under Dane, Norman, or Angevin, Englishmen were a subject race, conquered and ruled by foreign masters; and yet it was in these years of subjection that England first became really England. . . . The English Lords themselves sank into a middle class as they were pushed from their place by a foreign baronage who settled on English soil."

"In 800 A. D.," says Mr. West, in his modern history, revised edition, page 4, "Europe was still sunk deep in the barbarism that followed the long anarchy of the invasions, and the brief revival of Charlemagne had not gone far toward restoring civilisation. Schools and learning were almost extinct; commerce hardly existed; communication between district and district was almost impossible; money was so scarce that revenue had to be collected in produce; and manners and morals were alike deplorable." There has been hardly any period in the history of India about which anything so disparaging can be said. Again says Mr. West, "From 814 to about 1100, Europe had three centuries of 'Dark Ages,' caused by a new series of barbarian invasions and continued by 'feudal' violence of the local military organisation that society adopted to ward off these invasions." In fact Europe was in constant war right up to 1870, and the idea of nationhood had not developed till late in the nineteenth century. It is then not right to taunt the Indians with the absence of a perfected nationality in their country. Yet it can not be denied that the idea of nationhood is being developed pretty fast in India, even on modern lines. In fact I maintain that fundamentally India has been a nation for the last 2000 years, in spite of the fact that at times it has been divided into several kingdoms and principalities, sometimes under a common empire and in other times independent of each other.

But even if the worst happens and India is split up into a number of political units, what then? To me this does not appear to be so appalling as it may seem to others. Some Indians think that in any case it is better to be *men* fighting their own battles than to be mere *creatures* always in the leading strings of others. They have no faith in "peace at any price" or in "peace under any circumstances."

III

This book was written when I was travelling in the United States from January to May, 1915. It was ready for the press in June, 1915. Its publication has been delayed by causes which need not be stated.

Since then much has happened in India which bears upon the subject and might briefly be referred to here.

Early in 1915 something like organised anarchy and disorder broke out in the Southwestern districts of the Punjab, resulting in the free looting of many villages in several districts. This lawlessness was due to war. It is said that the police and the officers were overtaken by panic and order was not restored until strong measures were taken from the headquarters. About 4000 persons were arrested in connection with these disturbances and some 800 of them were sentenced to different terms of imprisonment, the rest being acquitted for want of evidence.

Towards the end of 1914 and in the first few months of 1915 the Punjab was the scene of many dacoities and murders, committed by and under the inspiration of Indians who had returned to India from abroad to take advantage of the war situation for political purposes. Some of these persons had gone from Canada; some from China; and some from the Pacific Coast of the United States. Amongst them were a large number of those who had been refused admission into Canada by the Canadian authorities and who had suffered enormously by their trip to Canada and back. The first clash between the latter and the Government took place at Budge Budge,[8] in Bengal, where the returned emigrants from Canada landed in order to proceed to their homes in the Punjab. The Gov-

[8] A town on the Eastern Coast of India.

ernment wanted to restrict their freedom of movement and would not let them go to Calcutta, whither a number of them wanted to proceed. These persons had concealed arms in their possession, and it appears that there was a free fight between them and the police, resulting in fatal casualties on both sides. About this time or a little later, the Government of India passed a special law, authorising officials to intern or imprison any person or persons in British India without trial, on mere suspicion of his or their being dangerous to the tranquillity of the country. Under this law they began to intern a large number of those who had returned from Canada and the United States and other places outside India, until the number reached to thousands. Most of them, perhaps, were kept only under surveillance. Yet a good many of them managed to put themselves into communication with the revolutionary party in India and eventually organised a "widespread conspiracy" to subvert British rule. The Government discovered this conspiracy by means of spies, who entered into the designs of the conspirators as "*agents provocateurs.*" It appears from the evidence subsequently given before the special tribunal appointed to try those who were arrested in connection with this conspiracy, that their plans were laid out on a comprehensive scale, with everything organised in a perfect way; that full provision had been made for finances as well as arms, and that the army had been approached with more or less success at different places in Northern India. At first a batch of about 65 were placed for trial before the special tribunal consisting of two English judges and one Indian. This tribunal was formed under the special law referred to above, and its decision was to be final in the sense that no appeal could be made from it to any other superior court. The tribunal eventually found that the conspiracy was seditious in its nature, and but for its timely discovery would have resulted in "widespread disaster." The proceedings of the tribunal were not open to the public nor to the press. A brief report of the proceedings was issued from day to day under the authority of the tribunal. Some of the accused could not be found. Out of the 61 charged, only 4 were acquitted, 6 were sentenced to various terms of imprisonment, 27 to transportation for life,[9] and 24 to death.[10] Commenting on this trial, the Lieutenant Governor of the Punjab observed in the course of a speech made in the Punjab Legislative Council held on September 25, 1915, that "these crimes did all over the Central Punjab from November, 1914, to July, 1915, create a state not only of alarm and insecurity, but of terror and even panic, and if they had not been promptly checked by the firm hand of authority and the active co-operation of the people, would have produced in the province as was intended by the conspirators a state of affairs similar to that of Hindustan in the mutiny[11]— paralysis

[9] Some of these sentences have been reduced.

[10] In 16 cases these sentences have been commuted to lifelong imprisonment not out of mercy as the Viceroy has himself officially pointed out, but in consideration of the evidence.

[11] The great mutiny of 1857, of which more hereafter.

of authority, widespread terrorism and murder not only of the officers of the Government but of loyal and well disposed subjects." What is significant is, that the leader, Rash Behari Bose, a Bengalee, who had organised several such conspiracies, escaped. Commenting upon the same trial, the *Times of India,* an influential Anglo-Indian paper published in Bombay, remarked:

"If this conspiracy had been disclosed in ordinary times there might have been a tendency to regard the members as representative of a considerable class of India . . . but, as it is, the revolutionary party stands out a mere fraction of the population, a dangerous and determined section of the population perhaps, yet so small that it can not command any chance of success while the sentiment of the country remains what it has been so splendidly proved to be."

Commenting upon the severity of the sentences inflicted, the Indian press took occasion to point out the grievous wrongs under which the country suffered at the hands of the British. After the conclusion of this case, over 100 persons more were indicted at Lahore [11a] and a large number at Benares, in connection with the same conspiracy. Besides, a number of men belonging to the military were tried and convicted in different stations in Northern India.

In Bengal political crime was rampant in a viru-

[11a] Six of them have been sentenced to death, 45 to transportation for life, some to imprisonment and some have been acquitted.

lent form throughout 1915. The Bengalee revolutionaries have kept the Government pretty busy all along the line, murdering police officials, looting treasuries, and committing dacoities, sometimes under the very nose of the police in the heart of the metropolis, resulting occasionally in so-called pitched battles between the police and the revolutionaries. Numberless trials have been going on in special tribunals constituted under the Defense of India Act, as well as in the ordinary courts. Large numbers of persons have been punished and equally large numbers are still undergoing trial.

There was a serious rising in Singapore, which was eventually put down with the help of the Japanese and French troops, and in connection with which a good many European lives were lost. Similarly, men smuggling arms and seditious literature, or attempting to smuggle arms, or otherwise carrying on anti-British propaganda, have been discovered, arrested and held in Burma, Singapore, Hongkong, Shanghai and Ceylon. A large number of Indians are in internment in Hongkong. Two Indian revolutionaries were deported from Japan, at the instance of the British Government, and several have been, I hear, interned in Java by the orders of the Dutch Government. Har Dayal and several others have been active in Europe and Asia Minor. The Hindu revolutionaries in the United States have also been busy in their propaganda. It is said that the Germans have been helping the Indians with funds and arms. How far they did render any substantial help in this matter is not known, but the conclusion of the Lahore Special Tribunal, that it was known to the leaders of the "Gadar" party in San Francisco in 1914, that a war between the British and Germans was on the *tapis* in August of that year, appears to be without foundation. The Indians who left the United States in 1914 to organise a rebellion in India, were neither financed nor otherwise inspired by the Germans. They went of their own accord, with their own money and on their own hook. Some of them were men of means. It may be true, however, that the Germans have helped the Indian revolutionaries with money and arms since. So much about the revolutionaries.

IV

Now something about the activity of the other wing of the Indian nationalists. When the war started, all of them declared for England, some sincerely, others for reasons of expediency. All were influenced by hopes of advancing their cause. For a time the appreciation in England — in and out of Parliament — amply justified their expectations. The first shock came when the British War Office refused to accept the offers of the Indian students in British universities to enlist in the army or as volunteers. The same fate met the offers of educated Indians in India. The offers made by some native princes and in a few cases by other members of the aristocracy for personal service were accepted, otherwise no relaxation in favour of any Indian was made in the rules for enlistment in the regular army or in the volunteers. The following extracts from the two leading Indian dailies of Calcutta and Allahabad will explain what I mean. The *Bengalee* of Calcutta said:

"When the war suddenly broke out in Europe there was a great outburst of feeling in India to serve the Empire in any capacity. There was a widespread desire among the more ardent spirits in this country to fight in defence of the Empire, and in Bengal, at any rate, there was an eager rush to enlist as volunteers. These young men were willing to cast aside their attitude of aloofness from what was primarily England's concern. They set before themselves a new ideal, the ideal of national self-realisation. By their participation in this struggle they felt they would be fighting the battles of their own freedom. It was the highest tribute the Government could expect from the people of this country of their loyalty and devotion to the throne. But the chill air of official scepticism nipped the scheme in the bud. We were told at the time not to embarrass the Government in any way; but we still lived in hopes that some means might be devised which would enable our young men to participate in this struggle so that from comradeship in arms there might arise comradeship in life leading to the necessary elevation of our status in the Empire. But a bureaucracy, with its instinctive disregard of others' feelings and interests, not only threw cold water on this salutary scheme but applied its mind to forging new fetters of repression. Thus the Defense of the Realm Act came to be passed, which is far more drastic and stringent than the similar statute in England. Internments have since become the order of the day. The whole thing offers a painful illustration of the psychology of the bureaucratic mind in its endeavour to breed loyalty and prevent disaffection. For while the spontaneous offer of our people, which was the outcome of a generous impulse and of genuine sentiments of loyalty and devotion, has been refused, fresh doses of repression are being applied to the wound thus inflicted on the minds of the people. But the crisis is not yet over, nor has the rising tide of feeling in this country completely subsided. There is a demand for men, always for more men, at the front. It seems we can not have too many men or too much of munitions if we desire a crushing victory. All the factories of England — and every available factory has been utilised for the manufacture of munitions of war — are working at top speed for the production of powder and shells for cannon. As regards men, volunteers are pouring forth from Canada, Australia, New Zealand and the mother country itself, in fact from all parts of the British Empire, except India. Can any one say why this invidious distinction is yet maintained? Why, while gifts of every sort from us are gladly accepted, the most precious gift of all, that of personal service with all the attendant risk that it implies, continues to be so unwelcome? Lord Kitchener is still calling for men. Mr. Bonar Law's recent speech at Shrewsbury indicates that even conscription may have to be resorted to. Why not then accept the offers of our men? The regular troops in the fighting line have earned no end of praise from the highest authorities for the display of their martial qualities. The Ambulance Corps shows the latest potentialities in our young men that are capable of development under proper guidance and training. We have not the slightest doubt that our volunteers would prove themselves equally fit and capable, no matter what the duties they are called upon to discharge. This war is said to be a war of democracy against militarism and autocracy, a holy war of justice and righteousness against the violation of international morality and the independence of small nations. Are these assertions strictly consistent with the refusal of our loyal offer, which also amounts to a denial of our equality of status with the rest of the Empire? If, during the heat of the war and in the midst of the crisis, there be yet observed and maintained this patent inequality of treatment and this assertion of racial superiority, how can we expect that they will be altogether forgotten or cast aside after the war when the readjustment comes to be made? Repression, we repeat for the hundredth time, is a disintegrating force. It alienates sympathies, destroys union and throws people into camps. Co-operation on the other hand is a healing and a cementing principle. But without equality of treatment there can not be any co-operation, and without co-operation there can not be any prospect of permanent peace. By accepting our offer the Government may give an earnest of future reforms and concessions. It will sensibly ease and improve the situation both here and at the front. But bureaucracy has so far failed to realise the situation and avail itself of the opportunity. Let not the words 'too late' be written by the future historian, regarding the action of the bureaucracy in this chapter of the history of India. . . . India wants equality of status with the rest of the Empire, and as a means to this end her sons want to fight as volunteers in this war; and if what Burke has said be true of Englishmen, neither the one nor the other of India's claims can be justly denied to her."

In its issue of September 8, 1915, the *Leader*, of Allahabad, said:

"The not unkindly critics of John Bull have often remarked that he has got a stolid temperament and an unemotional nature. The occasions are few and far between when he allows himself to be swayed by any strong outburst of passion. One such exception to this general course of conduct was furnished last year at the outbreak of the war. . . . When Lord Hardinge wired to England the message of India, her ungrudging and whole-hearted response to the call of the hour, its announcement in the House of Commons touched the deepest chords in the hearts of Englishmen. Then, for once, they let themselves go. There was almost a storm of English emotion. Even the *Times* thought that it foreshadowed a great change in the relations of India and England. 'Asiaticus' joined the chorus and swelled the pæan of the praise of Indian loyalty. He recanted his words of former days. He even praised Mr. Tilak. Mr. Roberts spoke of a change in the angle of vision. Other statesmen and other papers uttered the same language of joy and hope. All this naturally raised the hopes of India. Some, more imaginative than others, conjured up visions of glory. They imagined they could see the distant gleam of self-government. Others again, with a less imaginative nature, thought that even if self-government was still a far-off dream, they might yet see better days. The landing of Indian troops on the European soil was the signal for the outburst of another demonstration of feeling. Their heroic deeds, their unquestioning devotion to duty, formed the theme of sketch writers and leader writers in the English press. And yet to any one who has closely followed the course of events during the last six or seven months and studied the writings of the English press and the utterances of notable Englishmen in England and India, nothing is more clear than that an ominous reserve has again overtaken the English mind. Mr. Bonar Law talks of a consultation with the colonies, and forgets the very existence of India. Mr. Austen Chamberlain, since the day he assumed his office, has put a seal on his lips, and, whatever may flow beneath the surface from Downing Street to Delhi or Simla, nothing has fallen from his lips that can inspire confidence or kindle hope. The House of Lords have already given their reply to a sympathetic Viceroy, when, in the name of avoiding controversial issues, they shelved the question of an Executive Council for these provinces, which is another way of saying that they strangled it. Lord Curzon, Lord MacDonnel and Lord Sydenham are not likely to learn the wisdom which the force of events would teach to more plastic minds. If Indian students in England approach the higher authorities with a prayer that they may be admitted to the Officer's Training Corps, they are told to wait — indefinitely. If Sir George Scott Robertson, with imprudent enthusiasm, suggests the creation of an Indian guard, he is roundly told that he is impatient. 'Asiaticus' has again frankly gone back upon his short-lived liberalism, and Sir Valentine Chirol is no better. Convenience suggests the postponement of discussion of the Indian Budget, and the statute allows it. Out here in India the doctrine of unconditional loyalty is held up to us. We are told that it is a folly, if not a crime, to talk of what may come to India when the time for readjustment comes. Meanwhile Indian speculation, so natural to a nation of speculators, is roaming free. Hopes spring up only to give place to fears. . . .

"There are not wanting men among us also who have only one counsel to give, and that is, wait and see. No doubt the virtues of patience are great, but we think that so far as patience alone is concerned India may easily throw out a challenge to any nation in the world. If India will not help herself she will have little reason to grumble if others will not help her. Let us distinctly tell England that the time for half measures and gingerly reform has gone and that for bold and courageous steps has come."

V

The Indian National Congress, the official organisation of the constitutional party, held its annual session at Madras in December, 1914. In the course of his speech, the President remarked:

"If English rule in India meant the canonisation of a bureaucracy, if it meant perpetual domination and perpetual tutelage, and increasing dead-weight on the soul of India, it would be a curse to civilisation and a blot on humanity."

Again he asks complainingly:

"The right to carry arms, the right to bear commissions in the Army and lead our men in the cause of the Empire, the right to form volunteer corps in the defence of hearth and home, how long will these be denied to the Indian people? How long will India toddle on her feet, tied to the apron-strings of England? It is time she stood on her own legs. If England were obliged, as was Imperial Rome in her day, to abandon India in the hour of some great danger, what could be more humiliating to England and to India alike, than for India to be left unarmed and untrained in the use of arms, as her civil population now is, a prey to internal anarchy and external aggression? What a commentary would it be, on 150 years of British rule in India, that England found the people strong though disunited and left them helpless and emasculated?"

At Christmas, 1915, the Congress again met under the presidency of Sir S. P. Sinha, who was in 1908 the first Indian appointed to be a member of the Governor General's Executive Council, the British Cabinet in India. In the words of an Indian magazine, the speech delivered by him as coming from a man who has obtained "wealth, high position and honour" from the British connection and who has been "in the inner Councils of the Government," is most significant in its ideals as well as demands. His ideal of a government for India has been borrowed from Abraham Lincoln of the United States, viz., "Government of the people, *by the people,* for the people." He says:

"What I do say is that there should be a frank and full statement of the policy of Government as regards the future of India, so that hope may come where despair holds sway and faith where doubt spreads its darkening shadow, and that steps should be taken towards self-government by the gradual development of popular control over all departments of Government and by removal of disabilities and restrictions under which we labour both in our own country and in other parts of the British Empire."

Among the definite reforms and remedial and progressive measures which he demands are:

"Firstly — The grant of commissions in the army and military training for the people.

"Secondly — The extension of local self-government.

"Thirdly — The development of our commerce, industries and agriculture."

Regarding the first he goes into details as follows:

"1st. We ask for the right to enlist in the regular army, irrespective of race or province or origin, but subject only to prescribed tests of physical fitness.

"2nd. We ask that the commissioned ranks of the Indian army should be thrown open to all classes of His Majesty's subjects, subject to fair, reasonable and adequate physical and educational tests, and that a military college or colleges should be established in India where proper military training can be received by those of our countrymen who may have the good fortune to receive His Majesty's commission.

"3rd. We ask that all classes of His Majesty's subjects should be allowed to join as volunteers, subject of course to such rules and regulations as will ensure proper control and discipline, and

"4th. That the invidious distinctions under the Arms Act should be removed. This has no real connection with the three claims, but I deal with it together with the others as all these disabilities are justified on the same ground of political expediency."

As to the reasons why we should have self-government, he said:

"A British Premier early in this century very truly observed, 'Good government can not be a substitute for self-government.' Says a recent writer in a well-known British periodical, 'Every Englishman is aware that on no account, not if he were to be governed by an angel from heaven, would he surrender that most sacred of all his rights, the right of making his own laws. . . . He would not be an Englishman, he would not be able to look English fields and trees in the face, if he had parted with that right. Laws in themselves, have never counted for much. *There have been beneficent despots and wise law-givers in all ages who have increased the prosperity and probably the contentment and happiness of their subjects but yet their government has not stimulated the moral and intellectual capacity latent in citizenship or fortified its character or enlarged its understanding. There is more hope for the future of mankind in the least and faintest impulse towards self-help, self-realisation, self-redemption, than in any of the laws that Aristotle ever dreamt of.*[12] The ideal, therefore, of self-government is one that is not based merely on emotion and sentiment, but on the lessons of history."

What is, however, most significant, is his reply to the criticism often made by ignorant and prejudiced Englishmen and others as to what would be the fate of India if England were to withdraw from India and as to the Indians' fitness to manage their affairs or to fight their battles. He observes:

"I take leave to point out, therefore, that it is not correct, at any rate at the present time, to assert of any sections of the Indian people that they are

[12] The italics are mine.

wanting in such physical courage and manly virtues as to render them incapable of bearing arms. But even if it were so, is it not the obvious duty of England so to train them as to remove this incapacity, especially if it be the case, as there is some reason to believe, *that it is English rule which has brought them to such a pass?* England has ruled this country for considerably over 150 years now, and surely it cannot be a matter of pride to her at the end of this period that the withdrawal of her rule would mean chaos and anarchy and would leave the country an easy prey to any foreign adventurers. There are some of our critics who never fail to remind us that if the English were to leave the country to-day, we would have to wire to them to come back before they got to Aden. Some even enjoy the grim joke that were the English to withdraw now, there would be neither a rupee nor a virgin left in some parts of the country. I can conceive of no more scathing indictment of the results of British rule. A superman might gloat over the spectacle of the conquest of might over justice and righteousness, but I am much mistaken if the British nation, fighting now as ever for the cause of justice and freedom and liberty, will consider it as other than discreditable to itself *that after nearly two centuries of British rule India has been brought to-day to the same emasculated condition as that of the Britons in the beginning of the fifth century*[13] when the Roman legions left the English shores in order to defend their own coun-

[13] The italics are mine.

try against the Huns, Goths and other barbarian hordes."

The reader may well compare this with the following observation made by the present writer in a pamphlet [14] recently issued by him on the political situation in India.

" The whole world is free to keep arms and use arms. Every civilised nation is interested in giving a military training to her boys and citizens and in teaching them the use of arms and other military tactics. Some countries do this by conscription, others do it on a voluntary basis. No government entitled to be called sane thinks of denying arms to such of its people as want to use them for legitimate purposes. The free possession of arms and free training in military tactics for purposes of individual and national defence is the birthright of every son of a mother. Even the Amir of Kabul does not deny that to his people. Nations are vying with each other in their military preparations and in giving military training to their citizens. Even China is thinking of introducing conscription. In Japan military training is compulsory. In some places even the girls learn the use of arms and practise fencing. In the United States as well as in the other States of America the negroes and the American Indians can keep arms and receive military training. But the Indians of India can not keep arms. Every nation is interested in the manufacture of arms and ammunition and in inventing

[14] Some Reflections on the Political Situation in India, by Lajpat Rai, pp. 24-27.

effective methods of dealing with their enemies. Governments give every encouragement to those who invent new arms or improve old ones. All this is denied to the Indians.[15] Why? Because they are a subject people. Their government cannot trust them. The strength of the native army in India cannot exceed a certain proportion of the British army; they cannot handle the artillery; and numerous other restrictions are imposed upon the possession and use of arms by them. Why? Are they not fit to handle arms? Are they not brave? Are they intemperate? None of these things can be said of them. Yet no Indian can get a commissioned rank, however high by birth or social position, however fit by education. No Indian can be admitted into a military college in India or in Great Britain. Why? Are they unfit, or intellectually and physically imbeciles? The truth is that the Government of India, not being their *own* government, they cannot be trusted. They can be enrolled as mere soldiers and that only in certain numbers. Beyond that they cannot get any military training or military rank. Nor can the civil population be trusted to keep arms, much less to

[15] The ludicrous extent to which the prohibition to keep and use arms has been carried will be better illustrated by the following incident reported by the *Bengalee* of Calcutta.

"A five year old boy of Munshi Ganj Road, Kidderpore, had a toy pistol purchased for one anna. On the 8th of August last the child was playing with it but could not explode the paper caps. A thirteen year lad showed him how to do it. The boy was at once arrested by a beat constable and marched off to the Wat Ganjthana with the fire arm. The boy was eventually sent up for trial at Alipur and the Court fined him three rupees."

manufacture them. Much fuss has been made over the Indians having been allowed to participate in the European War. The Indians have gone mad over the incident, as if that were the greatest boon that could be conferred on them. The truth is that the step was actuated by and taken purely in British interests. Without the Indian contingent Great Britain could not send a decent expeditionary force to France. The whole of the white army could not be removed from India. In removing large numbers of them, it was necessary to remove proportionately large numbers of the native army also. The British Government is always distrustful of the native army. No amount of false statements and fallacious reasoning can conceal the fact that the British in India cannot allow the Indians to manufacture or carry arms, cannot give them a military training, cannot even keep a large native army (more than double the strength of the permanent British garrison) because, being foreigners, they cannot trust them. They fear that some day the arms or military training given them may be used against themselves. Looking at it from their point of view, perhaps, it cannot be said that they may not be right. But then, why ask the Indians to accept the pretence that the Government is national, and that they are the equal subjects of the crown; why hide the truth and make false and hypocritical declarations to the contrary? The British know the weakness of their rule in India, and in the disarming of the people they see the best guarantee of the continuance of their own rule and power. In the matter of arms, the present situation in India is this. One may steal arms; one may smuggle them; one may illicitly purchase them, from those who have the freedom of possessing, for the purpose of committing crime, but one cannot have them for defending his life and property, or the life and honour of his family (wife, mother, sisters, and daughters).[16]

"It is this which gives awful power to the lawless portions of society and which explains the losses and hardships of those who have suffered from the depredations of the latter and are suffering from dacoities and robberies and murders in Bengal and Punjab and elsewhere. There are plenty of arms in the country for the criminal, but none for the peace-loving (who only want them for defensive purposes). All this because the Government of India is a foreign government which cannot trust its subjects and which does not believe in their loyalty. In the light of this fact, all talk about the extraordinary outburst of loyalty becomes stale. So long as this state of things continues, it is useless for the Government to expect that the people can accept it and treat it as if it was their own national government. Never before, since the introduction of British rule in India, was the sense of helplessness, that arises out of the consciousness

[16] Commenting on the annual report of the issue of licenses the Indian press have made similar statements. The *Punjabee* says "while the ruffians bent on crime have been able to secure fire arms by foul means, the law abiding section of the community have for the most part continued helpless owing to the difficulties of obtaining licenses for fire arms." See also *Bengalee* of the 6th Oct. 1915.

of being a disarmed people, brought home to the people of India so vividly and strongly as during the war. A new fear has dawned on the public mind. Suppose the British lose, we are lost, says the Indian. The Germans may come or the Russians or even the Amir of Kabul, we cannot even make a show of resistance. A people so helpless and dependent deserve to be despised by the world. The war has made the Indian feel that, as a British subject, he is really a despicable creature entitled to no consideration at the hands of the other people of the world. Even the negroes (whether in Africa or America) are much better placed than he is. The prayers of Indian C. I. E.'s and Rai Bahadurs and Khan Bahadurs notwithstanding, the British cannot be invincible forever. The time is to come when their prowess in arms will decay. What will then be the fate of India and Indians? Will they be transferred like sheep? If they are not actually transferred by agreement, the nation replacing the English as the world power will take possession of India. The very idea is disquieting and crushingly humiliating. But this is not the only circumstance which constantly reminds the Indian people that their Government is an alien Government, whose interest in them is only secondary."

I will give one more quotation on this subject, and this time from the speech of a Parsi gentleman of extremely moderate views. Says Mr. Wacha:

"In connection with this war there is one serious disappointment to which I cannot refrain from making reference in this place. Many an enlightened and intelligent person, irrespective of caste and creed, in every province of the Indian Empire, has applied, from the very date of the declaration of war, to go to the front and fight side by side with the soldiers of the regular Indian army. Even to-day thousands on thousands are willing and ready to take up arms in the great cause for which the Allies are fighting. But unfortunately, the permanent bureaucracy of the land has sternly, if politely, refused those applications, the why and the wherefore of which has never been made known. It is this attitude of the Government, in the midst of the great tragic crisis, that has caused the bitterest disappointment to which many a leading organ of public opinion has given full expression. Russia, which has millions of population but less numerous than that of India, has already raised and is still raising a popular army full of ardour and patriotism to overcome the forces of the modern Vandals who are such enemies of liberty and freedom. The British Colonies are similarly raising corps after corps to give succour to the mother country, but strange to say, that while millions in India are on the qui vive to offer their services, a kind of proscription has gone forth from the governing authorities that they shall not be enrolled. This is indeed an un-English attitude which is unreconcilable with the entire policy of British administration in every other part of the Empire. I am only echoing the universal sentiments and feelings of my countrymen when I venture to say in this place that the Rulers of India still seem to mistrust the people."

Comparing the policy of the British with Imperial Rome, Mr. Wacha concludes:

"We all devoutly hope that profiting by this great achievement, Great Britain will not deny any further to the Indian people the exercise of arms, *the want of which for so many years has led to their emasculation.*"[17]

This word "emasculation" affords the key to the situation in India from the purely Indian point of view. Political, physical and economic "emasculation" is the keynote of British rule there, and however they may cloak it with wrappings of pleasant and golden words, and however they may conceal it in finely woven sentences, like the cloven feet it emerges at almost every step. The *Modern Review* puts it well when it says:

"Under bureaucratic rule, India is the poorest, the most unhealthy and the most ignorant among civilised countries, and her poverty and unhealthiness are not diminishing, and education is spreading at a slower pace than that of the snail. The remedy is Home Rule."

There is another brief quotation which I will give, from the speech of the President of the last session of the Indian National Congress, viz., the one relating to the poverty of India. He says: "Whatever differences of opinion may exist as to whether India is growing richer or poorer under the British rule, there is none with regard to her

[17] The italics are mine.

extreme poverty. And there can never be political contentment without material prosperity, shared in by all classes of the people. What the District Administration Committee of Bengal quotes with approval as regards Bengal, that our industrial backwardness is a great political danger, applies in reality to the whole of India.

"No one will be disposed to question the fact of this amazing backwardness. *Rich in all the resources of nature, India continues to be the poorest country in the civilised world.*" [18]

VI

I do not propose to burden this preface with other complaints which the Indian politicians make against the British Government, but I can not refrain from giving one more quotation from my own pamphlet on the question of Education:

"Let us look at education in India. India has been under British rule now for a century and a half in some parts, for over a century in others, and for at least 65 years in the Punjab. Yet the percentage of illiteracy is well nigh 95 per cent., taking the whole of India. Greatest ignorance prevails among the peasantry and the military classes, the two great bulwarks of British rule in India. What has the Government done to educate these classes? Nothing. Some maintain that they have been deliberately kept out of education because, once educated, they may no longer be such willing tools as they are now.

[18] The italics are mine.

"Agriculture in India, as elsewhere, is the least paying of industries, and it is not at all strange that large numbers of sturdy Punjabees prefer to labour in other countries rather than rot on their farms in the Punjab. In the early years of British rule the educated and the trading classes flourished and became prosperous, but now they are thoroughly discontented. The native traders are no longer happy under British rule, (1) because the railways and foreign import and export offices dealing directly with the producer and the consumer have ruined their business, (2) because the facilities available to them in the early days of British rule have disappeared, (3) because the bureaucracy is always inciting the agricultural and military classes against them and heaping insults on their devoted heads both by word and deed. In almost every province, special legislation has been enacted professedly in the interests of the agricultural classes but really directed against the Indian trader or money lender. On the other hand, what has the Government done to open non-agricultural pursuits to them? Nothing. In the whole length and breadth of the country there is not a single technological institute. The private or aided technological institutes are called by that name only by courtesy. In these days of international trade there is no provision in any of the Indian universities for the teaching of modern languages. While Germans, Austrians, Italians, Americans and Japanese can learn Hindustanee and English in their own countries in order to further their trade with India, the Government of India has never given a thought to the necessity of making a provision for the teaching of German, French, Japanese, &c., to the Indians and of encouraging Indians to learn these languages. The best part of a boy's student life is compulsorily spent in acquiring excellence in the use of the English language. Indians are not supposed to know other languages or to trade with other countries, because the English do it for them. It is not the concern of the British to encourage the native to have direct commercial transactions with foreign countries. There is not a single place in India where an Indian student can do research work in chemistry or other sciences. While the country is full of mines, there is no place to learn mining. Hundreds of steamers come and go from Indian ports, but there is no place in India where an Indian youth can qualify himself even for the merchant marine, not to speak of the navy. In the whole of India with its splendid resources, there is not a single place where ships can be built. The Indian Government has never given a thought to these questions because they do not concern them, because they are not interested in the development of the indigenous industries and in raising the status of the people. They have done a lot to encourage the produce of raw materials necessary for their industries or for their food (cotton, wheat, oil, seeds, etc.), but almost nothing to encourage manufacturing industries. Originally they wanted to preserve the Indian markets for themselves only, but their policy of free trade stood in the way, and latterly the Germans and now the Japanese are sharing that market with them. But to teach the Indian to manufacture for his own consumption has never entered the thought of those responsible for the administration of India. Perhaps it is not right to say that it never entered their thought. They are too intelligent and shrewd not to know that they had not done their duty to India in these matters, but the interest of their own people was paramount and that they could not set aside.

"The British Government in India can not go in for universal elementary education, as there is danger of even greater disaffection resulting therefrom; they can not give technical education of a high order, as that might interfere with British industries; they can not protect Indian industries for the same reason; they can not provide for real high class commercial education with a teaching of foreign languages and a knowledge of seafaring and navigation, as they do not want the Indians to directly engage in oversea trade and contract relations with other nations. They can not protect and subsidise Indian industries, as that is opposed to free trade and detrimental to British industries. Yet they want the Indians to believe that the British Government in India is primarily conducted in the interests of India.

"The people of India must remain ignorant, illiterate and industrially and commercially dependent because that benefits England and is for the advantage of her people.

"But that is not all. The Government of India can not even provide for high class education in sciences, in engineering, and in medicine, for the simple reason that the higher positions in these professions they want to reserve for their own people. Of late the number of Indians, educated and trained in these departments of knowledge in British and other foreign universities, has so increased as to become rather embarrassing to the Government of India. They can not utilise them without reducing the number of Britishers in these services. This they do not desire. The result is that there are numbers of trained Indians in India with high class British and European qualifications who have to be contented with subordinate positions under Britishers of lesser qualifications, and perhaps, at times, of no qualifications. The competitive examinations for higher services are held in England, which in itself is a great injustice; but this year on account of the war, there being fewer qualified Britishers to compete for these services, the Government has resolved to discontinue [18a] some of the examinations, for fear lest a larger number of Indians than is desirable might get into them. Can they still say that the Government of India is as good as or perhaps better than a national government? The truth is that they do not want a larger number of Indians in the higher services because

[18a] The examinations have not been discontinued but statutory provision has been made for a large proportion of the appointments formerly filled by examination to be now filled by nomination.

they can not trust them. For the same reason they distrust private educational institutions and insist upon the employment of Britishers as inspectors of schools and as professors in the educational service. They will allow a certain number of Indians in the higher offices but that number must not be so large as to make it even remotely possible for them to create trouble for the Government. The same fear underlies the administration of local bodies and the constitution and powers of the Councils. It is simply begging the question to argue that Indians are not yet ready or fit for representative institutions. The real question is the dread of power passing from the Britishers into Indian hands.[19] It is this dread that is the dominating influence in the policy of the British Government in India. India is a possession and a dependency and must be administered in the best interests of the master. Many credulous Indians talk of the liberty-loving traditions of the British democracy, but they forget that the application of these traditions to India would make such big holes in their safes, purses, and incomes, that they as men swayed by self-interest and love of power and glory, can never think of enforcing these principles in India. The British are good people. In all personal dealings they are honest, frank, and reliable. But when national interests are at stake and when the interests of the

[19] Mr. Lowes Dickinson, an English Professor who has largely travelled in India, has practically admitted the truth of this remark. (P. 23, An Essay on the Civilisation of India, China, and Japan. See also pp. 27 and 28.)

nation dictate a different line of policy, they can not help following the latter, however much injustice and hardship they may inflict upon others in doing so. The English political moralist and thinker believes and preaches that the state exists for the people, that state and people are really interchangeable words, and that the teachings of Treitschke, that the state is greater than the people and that the latter exists for the former, is immoral and vicious. In Great Britain and the Colonies the British act as they believe, but in India they follow the doctrines of the German professor. The state in India is an authority imposed from without and is therefore distinct from and independent of the people.[20] The state in India is the British people, and therefore the interests of the latter must override those of the Indian people. Everything in India is judged by that standard. The English may be good, benevolent, just, kind, and fair-minded, but all these virtues are dominated by the supreme test mentioned above. All the real troubles of India arise from this circumstance. Everything connected with India is looked at from this angle. Unless this angle changes there is no possibility of any such changes taking place in the system and the policy of the Government of India as are likely to satisfy the self-respect of the Indian or to remove the disadvantages from which the country suffers."

[20] The *Pioneer* of Allahabad, a semi-official organ of the Anglo-Indians, has in a recent issue said that "The safety of the State is and must be of far greater importance than the rights of the individuals."

VII

The most significant development of Nationalism, however, that has taken place in the last year, is the unity between the Hindus and the Mohammedans on the question of self-government. It is remarkable how the war has united the Hindus and the Mohammedans, not only in their expressions of loyalty to the Government, but also in their demand for Home Rule and in their dissatisfaction with the prevailing political conditions in India. For the first time in the history of Indian Nationalism, the Indian National Congress and the All-India Muslim League have met in the same city. This was opposed with the whole of their might by the Ultra-Loyalists among the Mohammedans under the inspiration of their Anglo-Indian masters. The younger generation of the Mohammedans, however, is so thoroughly filled with the idea of Nationalism that they carried the day and succeeded in holding a very successful session of their league at Bombay in the same week in which the Indian National Congress was holding its session in that city. The result was that the members of both organisations met, compared notes, exchanged civilities, and found out that there was practical unity among them on all the important questions bearing upon their relations with the Government. The Muslim League President made pronouncements demanding self-government, free compulsory education, governmental help in industrial development, removal of restrictions against the progress of Indian industries, in almost the same terms and with the same emphasis, if not even greater, than the Indian National Congress did. Both the organisations appointed a joint committee to draw up a scheme of Home Rule which would meet the needs and the approval of both the great religious communities inhabiting that great country.

During the last year a scheme has been floated by Mrs. Annie Besant, the president of the Theosophical Society, a woman of great ability and of world-wide fame, who has adopted India as her home, but who at the same time is a patriotic Englishwoman, to organise a Home Rule League for India, separate from and independent of both the Indian National Congress and the All-India Muslim League. This proposal has met with the approval of the advanced members of both the Hindu and Mohammedan communities. Some leaders of the Indian National Congress, however, see a danger to their Congress in the growth and development of the Home Rule League. But it is wonderful how the idea has caught hold of the public mind. Practically the whole of the Nationalist press and the Nationalist platform, with a few minor exceptions, have declared in favour of the proposal. The supporters of the Home Rule League met at Bombay to formally decide the question of giving practical effect to the idea which has received the joint support of both the Hindus and the Mohammedans. Mrs. Besant, however, herself, has shrunk from organising it just now, out of deference to the opinions of some of the leaders of the Indian National Congress, pending the report of the joint committee formed to formulate a scheme of Home Rule suited to India. Indian Nationalism has thus advanced very much during the last year. We have the two movements — one representing force, the other peaceful agitation — side by side, as has been the case in the history of similar movements in other countries. One movement represents the more virile section of the population who believe in force, violence and terrorism; the other, those who depend upon appeal to reason, justice and conscience. The combined force of both, however, produces a momentum which is sure to become irresistible in the course of time. What is extremely hopeful is the entirely changed attitude of the Mohammedan community. The British wished for and tried to create an *Ulster* among the Mohammedans of India. They had well nigh succeeded, but the last three or four years have brought about a complete change. The Mohammedan masses had really never joined the educated Mohammedan Separatists, but even the latter have now found out that the policy of separation from the Hindus which was in their minds for some time, can not eventually bring any lasting good tc their community. With their Hindu countrymen they feel that India must occupy the first place in their affections and thoughts, and that it was not inconsistent for them to be Mohammedans in religion and Indians in politics. Similarly, the Hindu sentiment, that was growing somewhat anti-Mohammedan on account of the Mohammedan sentiment of separation, has been greatly softened. The Mohammedans have begun to feel that they can share in the ancient glory of India without an outrage to their Mohammedanism. The Hindus have come to realise that after all the Mohammedan rule in India was not so bad or tyrannical and oppressive as they were told it was by interested historians. The Mohammedans feel that they can be as proud of the Hindu heroes, Rama and Krishna, of the Hindu Epics, the Ramayana and the Mahabharta, of Hindu science and Hindu philosophy, as the Hindus themselves are, without being false to their religion or to their community. Similarly the Hindus feel that they can be as proud of a Sher Shah and an Akbar and a Shah Jahan, of Alberuni, of Ibn Batuta, of Abul Fazal, Faizi and Gálib, as the Mohammedans can be. Nay, they can go a step further and say that even Aurangzeb was not, after all, so bad as they had supposed him to be. The Hindus and Mohammedans have discovered that they can take part in their respective festivals and take pride in their respective past, without in any way being traitors to their respective religions and communities.

VIII

That the above statements are not mere creations of my own brain, but are based on fact, will be easily seen from the following extracts which I make from the speech of the President of the last session of the All-India Muslim League held at Bombay in December, 1915.

First, about the representative character of the assembly, Mr. Mazhar-ul-Haq remarked:

" Please accept my sincere and heartfelt thanks for the great honour you have done me by electing me the President of the All-India Muslim League this year. It is a proud privilege to preside over and guide the deliberations of this distinguished gathering, where representatives of seventy millions of his Britannic Majesty's Indian Muslim subjects are assembled in conference for the betterment of their condition, and for counsel and consultation together on the affairs of their country."

About the difficulties of the times he says:

" Times are most unpropitious for expressing views and convictions which, in normal times of peace, there would have been no harm in frankly and unreservedly putting *before our community and our Government.* The present terrible conflict of nations enjoins upon us the paramount duty of saying or doing nothing which would embarrass or weaken the hands of our Government by producing undesirable excitement in the people, or lead to any impression upon foreign nations that we are in any way inimical or even indifferent to the best interests of the Empire."

As to how Islam established itself in India, how it spread and what is the present position of the Mohammedans of India, he speaks as follows:

" The first advent of the Muslims in India was along these very coasts [21] in the form of a naval expedition sent by the third Khalif in the year

[21] The Western Coast.

636 A. D. This was more than four hundred years before William the Conqueror defeated the Saxons at the battle of Hastings. After many vicissitudes, into the details of which it is unnecessary to go, the Muslim Empire was firmly established in India. These invaders made India their home and did not consider it a land of regrets. They lived amongst the people of the country, mixed with them freely and became true citizens of India. As a matter of fact they had no other home but India. From time to time their number was strengthened by fresh blood from Arabia, Persia and other Muslim lands, but their ranks were swollen mainly by additions from the people of the country themselves. It is most interesting to know that out of the present seventy millions of the Muslim population, those who have claimed their descent from remote non-Indian ancestors amount only to eight millions. Whence have the remaining millions come, if not from Indian ranks? The Muslims enriched the hoary civilisation of India with their own literature and art, evolved and developed by their creative and versatile genius. From the Himalayas to Cape Comorin the entire country is studded with those gems of art which remind one of the glorious period of Muslim rule. The result was a new civilisation which was the outcome of the combined efforts of all the peoples of India and the product of the two great civilisations in the history of the world. During Muslim times all offices were equally opened to all, without any distinction of class, creed or colour. The only conditions were

fitness and efficiency. So we have the spectacle of a Hindu prime minister, a Hindu commander-in-chief, a Hindu finance minister, and a Hindu governor of Kabul. Ethnology and folklore of India speak eloquently of manners and customs showing the influence of one people upon the other. The only link which the Muslims kept with the countries outside India was the spiritual link of their religion. This was under the circumstances inevitable. This short historical retrospect may be succinctly expressed in two words which fully and clearly describe the elements and conditions of our existence in India. We are Indian Muslims. These words, 'Indian Muslims,' convey the idea of our nationality and of our religion, and as long as we keep our duties and responsibilities arising from these factors before our eyes, we can hardly go wrong.

"Indian Muslims are Indians first!

"About what we owe to our non-Muslim fellow subjects I have never concealed my opinion, and I can only repeat here what I have often said. I am one of those who have never taken a narrow and sectarian view of Indian politics. When a question concerning the welfare of India and of justice to Indians arises I am not only an Indian first, but an Indian next and an Indian to the last, an Indian and an Indian alone, favouring no community and no individual, but on the side of those who desire the advancement of India as a whole without prejudice to the rights and interests of any individual, much less of any community, whether my own or another.

" Policies and principles of a nobler kind may be laid down by higher authorities, but their value is determined by those who have to carry them out. Thus it has often been the case in India that noble intentions have degenerated into pious wishes and even into harmful actions. If the Indian people were real partners in the actual governance of the country, the Indian point of view would have prevailed, much that is now admitted to have been mistaken would have been avoided, the country would have progressed and the ruling classes would have been spared the bitter and sometimes undeserved criticisms hurled against them. Unless and until India has got a national government and is governed for the greatest good of the Indian people, I do not see how she can be contented. India does not demand 'a place in the sun' in any aggressive sense, but she does require the light of the Indian sun for her own children.

" Gentlemen, let us descend a little from the generalities into details and see how the policy of the past has worked not only to our detriment, but to the positive weakening of the British rule itself. Let us see what small share we have in the larger life of the Empire. I have already said that we have no share in laying down the policy upon which India is ruled. Have we any share even in the different Services of the country? Are we allowed to serve our own land and the Empire to the best of our capacity and ability? In every country the three premier Services are considered to be the Military, the Naval and the Diplomatic.

"Let us begin with the Military. In spite of the numerous martial races who inhabit India in millions, no Indian can rise above the non-commissioned ranks. We can not hope to gain a higher position than that of a Subadar-Major or a Risaldar-Major. Every position that would give us an independent command is closed to us. The regular army is limited in number, no volunteers are taken from our ranks and the general population is rigorously disarmed. The Arms Act perpetuates invidious distinctions on grounds of colour and creed — distinctions most humiliating to the people of the country. Going about their ordinary daily occupations our people may be attacked by dacoits and evilly disposed persons or even by wild beasts, but they can not defend themselves. Even *lathis*[22] have been held by some judicial authorities to be dangerous weapons. Newspapers and official communiques tell us that ordinary Naiks of our Indian Army have on the battlefield conducted themselves most bravely and have led their companies with conspicuous gallantry and ability at times when all the English officers were either killed or disabled. If our men are capable of such initiative and valiant deeds on the actual field of battle, why, Indians naturally ask, should they not be trusted in the piping times of peace? Had they only been trained and allowed to serve, millions and millions would have sprung to the side of England at her slightest call in this, the hour of her need. Indeed, no other nation of the world has such an inexhaustible

[22] Heavy wooden sticks.

source of strength as Great Britain has in the teeming masses of India, but India has been so maimed and crippled in her manhood that she can help neither herself nor Great Britain. The idea is galling and humiliating that, if a time came when India was in danger, her own sons would not be able to save their hearths and homes, or the honour and lives of their wives and children, but would have to look to foreign nations like Japan and Russia for help and succour. Peace and order are the first requisites of a settled government and without them there would be mere chaos; but unlimited and long-continued peace has a tendency to enervate and emasculate people. To make a living nation, higher qualities are required. A spirit which will not bow before any adverse wind, an internal strength which will bear all toils and troubles, a determination which will flinch from no task, however impossible it may appear, a discipline which will love and be happy in the service of the country and the Empire, are qualities necessary for the attainment of that life which I call a full life. These moral forces can only come into play when people are free and unrestricted in the exercise of all their faculties. The profession of arms is perhaps one which breeds this spirit and brings out these potential forces more than any other. To close it to any portion of humanity is to turn them into lifeless machines.

"In the Navy, we cannot rise above the rank of a lascar. Attempts are often made to keep us out even of this lowly position. India has a vast seaboard, peopled by seafaring nations. To refuse them their birthright is to waste so much good material which would have gone to increase the strength of the Empire. Why not have a few Indian dreadnaughts and cruisers manned by Indians and commanded by their own countrymen? It is said that the Indians are not fit for the Navy. Having not trained and tried them, it is not just or fair to say so. Try them first and, if found wanting, then you have a right to reject them. The history of ancient India proves that naval capacity is here; but it lies dormant for want of sufficient opportunity.

"Now I pass on to the Diplomatic Service. Here we are conspicuous by our entire absence from it. What prevents the Government from utilising the intellect, the ability and the energy of our people in this direction, I fail to understand. Why should not some of the numerous posts of Political Residents and Agents of India be opened to them?

"In India, the Civil Service is considered to be the premier public service of the country. Here, too, we are circumscribed and hedged in by rules and regulations which make it for our people, if not altogether impossible, at least very difficult to enter. The examination which is the only possible way of entry for an Indian is held in London, 7,000 miles away from his home. Those educated youths who can not bear the cost and expenses of such a journey, are entirely debarred from it, however brilliant they may be. The fortunate few, who can afford to compete with Englishmen, have to do so in a language absolutely foreign to them. Why the examinations should not be held both in England and India to give the youths of both countries equal chances is an anomaly which passes my comprehension. For a number of years the country has been loudly demanding this much delayed justice, but instead, we get the recent Indian Civil Service Act which has entirely abolished the competitive system. No doubt the operation of the Act is temporary, but a wrong precedent has been created, and no one knows to what further developments it will lead.

"In the minor services of the country, such as Police, Forest, Education, the higher places have been reserved for Europeans and the children of the soil have been told that the doors have been shut against them. One would have expected that at least in these minor places Indians would not have failed, but all our protests and entreaties have been of no avail so far.

"Gentlemen, I pass on now to the economical development of the country. Let us see what progress we have made in this direction. Admittedly India is an agricultural country and its real life and strength is in the teeming millions of humanity who live in the villages, principally by agriculture. Has anything really been done to raise them from their poverty-ridden and helpless condition? In spite of the jugglery of figures in which the hearts of statisticians delight, what is the state of the country and its peasantry? Statistics are supposed to prove every theory advanced by men anxious to prove their case, but our eyes are our best witnesses and can not deceive us. India is a country rich in natural resources — resources which are not inferior to any other country in this wide, wide world. Her land bears every variety of crops from cotton and jute to wheat and mustard. Her mines produce every kind of metal from gold and iron ores down to the best coal, and not excluding numerous precious stones. She has a climate ranging from the bitterest cold to the intensest heat. Her rivers and forests are full of life and materials useful to man. In short, India is a self-contained, miniature world. In such a country what is the condition of her inhabitants? No toil or trouble is spared for the cultivation of their fields by the wretched and over-worked peasantry. All that manual labour can do is done, but because of the want of scientific methods and other causes beyond their control, the profits which ought to have been theirs are lost to them. Side by side with green, minutely and industriously cultivated fields, we find tiny and dilapidated mud hovels thatched with old and rotten straw. In these hovels there are neither windows nor floor-cloths, and the only furniture that they boast of is a few earthen vessels and perhaps a *chatai*.[23] Human beings and cattle herd together with no arrangements for sanitation. Such are the conditions in which the great majority of our people pass their miserable existence.

"In commerce and industry we are no better off. Our old indigenous industries have been killed by

[23] A straw mat.

foreign competition and new attempts are crippled in the interests of other peoples than those of India. The instance of the cotton excise duties is before us — duties which have been imposed in the interests of Manchester and Lancashire.

"I now pass on to two of the recent repressive measures, the Press Act and the Defence of India Act. These acts have worked harshly and told heavily upon the persons and the properties of some leaders of our community. Musalmans are intensely agitated, and I should be grossly negligent in the discharge of my duties as the spokesman of Muslim India, if I failed to give voice to their feelings on the subject. On principle and by sentiment I object to repression and coercion, be it from the Government or from any section of a disaffected people.

"I remember well, how and under what conditions the Press Act was passed. The members of the Imperial Council gave their consent to the passing of the bill on the express understanding that the law was intended for the anarchists and would never be applied in the case of peaceful citizens anxious to enlighten Government officers as to the sentiments and feeling of the people. But what is the result? *All the independent Muslim papers have either been wiped out or are dragging on a lifeless and miserable existence.*[24] The *Comrade* is gone, *The Hamdard* has been strangled to death, the *Muslim Gazette* ceased to exist long ago, *Al-Hilal* is no more, the *Zamindar* is carrying on its colour-

[24] The italics are mine.

less existence with a sword of Damocles always hanging over its head. Whoever thought that the Press Act would be applied in this fashion? Is it possible for the people not to resent such treatment and are their feelings to be treated so lightly?"

The reader will notice that there is nothing in this book which is in any way stronger either in language or in sentiments than what the President of the All-India Muslim League has said in the quotations given above. Along with these expressions of discontent are also found in his address very strong declarations of loyalty to the Government and of appreciation of what they have done for India. The task of appraising the exact value of both kinds of statements may better be left to the reader.

This is the dawn of a new day in India which the British will have to reckon with. We know that they are very skilful in *divide et impera,* but the Indian people are now awake and that policy may not succeed so well in the future as it has in the past.

The Indians have no desire to do anything which might in any way injure or harm the position of Great Britain as a world power. They would much rather gain Home Rule in India by peaceful means and remain a part of the British Empire than subvert British authority in India by force or seek the assistance of any other foreign power to gain their end. But in case the British continue to trample upon their rights and to humiliate them and to exploit them as they have done in the past, then there is no knowing what they might not be tempted or forced to do. What is clear is this, that the number of such Indians is growing larger and larger every day who are willing and ready to sacrifice their careers, their prospects, their happiness and their life at the altar of what they consider to be their duty to their country.

There are others who think that their patience has been well nigh exhausted; who can not wait and would strike for their liberty at once, saying "Our trust is in God."

IX

Before concluding this introductory part of my study of the Nationalist Movement in India, I desire to tender my heartfelt thanks to Professor A. U. Pope, of the University of California, for the encouragement and advice he has given me in the preparation of this book, and to Dr. J. T. Sunderland, of New York, for having read my manuscript and written a Foreword for me.

The reader will, I hope, excuse me for certain repetitions. They are unavoidable in a book of this kind, where it is desirable to show that the different communities and classes of the Indian population think on the same lines in national affairs.

Lastly, I have to beg the pardon of the reader for certain personal references which may seem to be self-laudatory. I have indulged in this weakness only when it was absolutely necessary for the continuance of the thread of the narrative. In one chapter I have retained the third person singular so as to avoid being understood that I was speaking of myself.

I am also conscious of the meagreness of certain chapters. The book is too short to be called a History of the National Movement. It is written more with the object of drawing the attention of the civilised world to what is happening in India, than to prepare a complete record of the movement. The foreign reader can not be expected to be interested in details. Moreover, he may never read a long and expensive book. Hence the studied brevity kept in view all through. Nor do I propose to discuss the fitness of Indians for immediate self-government as that would largely add to the bulk of the book, but for a brief and able discussion of the matter I may refer the reader to an article by the Editor in the *Modern Review* of Calcutta for February, 1916.

Then again it is to be regretted that the illustrations are so few. I would have liked to add many more. Many prominent Nationalists find no place for the simple reason that at the time of sending the book to the press I have not been able to get their pictures. Originally there was no idea of having any illustrations. It is too late now to delay the publication of the book pending the receipt of pictures from India. Indeed the mail facilities, just now, are so dubious that one can not be certain of getting them at all so long as the war lasts.

LAJPAT RAI.

Berkeley, California, U. S. A.,
1st of March, 1916.

YOUNG INDIA

AN INTERPRETATION AND A HISTORY OF THE NATIONALIST MOVEMENT FROM WITHIN

CHAPTER I

THE GENERAL VIEWPOINT OF THE INDIAN NATIONALIST

INDIAN History rolls back to thousands of years before the Christian Era. Much of it is still enveloped in mystery. What little is known has been discovered and put in shape within the last hundred years. The materials, from which the early History of India has been prepared, have long been in existence, but little of them were known to the Western people.

It can not be said that a complete history of Ancient India has been fully and finally constructed. What is known has been discovered bit by bit. Much yet remains to be found and put in order. It is quite unsafe, therefore, to dogmatise about the deficiencies of Ancient Indian civilisation. Yet this much can be said with certainty, that centuries before the birth of Christ India possessed a marvellous civilisation, a wonderful literature, a well organised social system, a conception of government based on law and on the legal rights of subjects *intcr se*, as well as against the ruling monarch.[1]

We have, besides, ample evidences in the ancient literature of India, as translated and interpreted by Western scholars, to the effect that democratic institutions were not unknown to Ancient India.[2] Nor can it be said that the idea of universal sovereignty over the whole of India under one permanent power was unknown to the Hindus. How often it was realised and for how long, can not be said with any certainty.[3]

First Invasion of India. The first political and military invasion of India known to history was that of Alexander the Great in 326 B. C. Alexander was no doubt victorious up to a certain point, but he never conquered India, nor did he occupy it. He did not reach even so far into the interior as Delhi on the Jumna. He is said to have left behind him some officers to administer the affairs of the conquered province, but it is a well established historical fact that in the conflict between Chandra Gupta, the Hindu, and Seleucus, the Greek, who was the chief ruling authority in Babylon after the death of Alexander, Seleucus was practically worsted and a peace was concluded by which the independence of India was fully realised. Chandra Gupta ruled over the whole of India north of

[1] "The Raja (*i. e.*, the king) was not above the law." See Wilson's note on p. 203, vol. I of Mill's British India.

[2] See Rhys David's "Buddhist India."

[3] See an account of Yudhishthira's *Rajsuya yajna* in the Mahabharata.

Vindhyachal. Bengal as far east as Assam, and the Punjab as far west as Afghanistan, were among his provinces. Fortunately for us, we have enough independent testimony in the writings of Megasthenes, the Greek Ambassador at the court of Chandra Gupta, and other contemporaneous Greek writers, as to the state of India at that time.

Chandra Gupta and Asoka. Megasthenes' account of the Government of Chandra Gupta and of the details of the administration under him, is enough to fill every Indian with pride. Chandra Gupta's organisation[4] included almost every form of governmental activity known to modern Europe. There was a separate department of labour under him, a separate registrar of births, deaths and marriages, a minister who looked after public charities, another in charge of trade and commerce, one in charge of agriculture, and so on. He had a great army, a currency and a navy. Even then the system of commercial papers was well known to Indians, who had a great name for honesty and truthfulness. Their word was better than a bond. Chandra Gupta was followed by Asoka, perhaps the greatest and noblest Emperor India has had during the historical period. Under him the whole country was consolidated under one imperial sway. He ruled not by force, but by love. His love extended even to animals. He is known to have organised hospitals for the treatment of animals. All this happened before Christ was born. Between 326

[4] For an account of Chandra Gupta's Government see Early History of India by Mr. Vincent Smith.

B. C. and the middle of the eighth century A. D., India knew no foreign masters, in the sense that it was never ruled for any length of time from without. A few of the nomadic tribes of Central Asia did penetrate into India, only to be absorbed and assimilated by the mass of the Aryans already settled and in power there.

The next foreign invasion of India, which was to leave a permanent mark on the history and institutions of India and with which starts an altogether separate epoch in Indian history, was by Abul Qasim in the middle of the eighth century. For full 400 years the Mohammedans knocked at the door of India before they could establish a kingdom there. The first Mohammedan King of Delhi was Kutb-ud-din Aibak, who established a dynasty in 1206 A. D. The Mohammedans were in possession of some parts of Sindh and the Punjab between the eighth and the twelfth centuries, but India was not conquered nor the Hindus beaten until Prithvi Raj, the last Rajput King of Delhi, was defeated by the treachery of a brother Rajput chief in the year 1193 A. D.

India Practically Independent up to the Twelfth Century. It will be thus seen that India was practically independent up to the beginning of the thirteenth century A. D. By independent, I mean that no foreign rule had been imposed upon it from without. Some parts of the northwestern provinces of the Punjab and Sindh had been for some time under Muslim domination, but the main territory was under native rulers and native laws. As said before, the tribes that overran the northwestern parts of India between the invasion of Alexander the Great and that of Abul Qasim, came to settle. Once settled there, they adopted the religion and the social life of the country and were merged with the natives. Thenceforth there was no distinction between them and the other Indian people.

Muslim Rule. The Mohammedan rule over India lasted for six centuries with varying vicissitudes of fortune. For three centuries, from the thirteenth to the beginning of the sixteenth century, their rule was practically confined to Northern India. Deccan, Rajputana and Central India were always more or less independent until Akbar consolidated the whole country under his flag; though even he failed to vanquish Partap, the invincible Rana of Udeypore (Rajputana).[5] Partap was defeated, was driven out of his capital, was pursued and harassed, but he did not make his submission to the Mogul. Akbar won over to his side almost all the other Rajput chiefs, some by his prowess, others by friendship, but the Sessodia[6] chief would not bend his knee. His countrymen simply worshipped him. So strong was the feeling of patriotism and the love of independence among the Hindus, even then, that when Akbar one day announced in the Durbar that he had received

[5] It is true that parts of Deccan had been from time to time overrun by the Mohammedans and at least one Muslim kingdom had been founded there even before Akbar's time, but still the general statement in the text stands good.

[6] The tribal name of the House to which Partap belonged.

a petition of submission from Partap, the Rajputs present in the Durbar refused to believe him. It is well known how one of them, Prithvi Raj, a poet, wrote to Partap of the indescribable grief the report had caused them, and telling him that the Hindu sun would set forever if Partap would yield; and how he received an answer that the report was wrong and that Partap would never yield and would keep the flag flying. That shows how a Hindu servant of Akbar, who had made his submission and accepted the service of the Mogul, felt in the matter. Although beaten himself, he would not acknowledge that the Hindus had been finally beaten so long as Partap was resisting the Mogul arms. It speaks very highly of the broad-mindedness of Akbar that, so far back as the sixteenth century, he allowed one of his Hindu captives and servants to speak out so boldly and plainly of his love of Hindu independence. Akbar, we must remember, had succeeded in making alliances with almost all the other important Rajput houses. The proud Rahtores[7] had given him a daughter for a bride, and the *Kutchwahas*,[7] Bikanir[7] and Boondi[7] had also submitted. So Partap had to fight the combined forces of Akbar and his own brother-Rajput chiefs, some of whom were related to him by the dearest ties of blood and marriage. Yet single-handed, for a quarter of a century, did he withstand the efforts of the mighty empire over which Akbar ruled to force his submission. In the words

[7] Names of Rajput ruling families in Akbar's time.

of Colonel Tod, it is worthy "the attention of those who influence the destinies of states in more favoured climes to estimate the intensity of feeling which could arm Partap to oppose the resources of a small principality against the then most powerful empire in the world, whose armies were more numerous and far more efficient than any ever led by the Persians against the liberties of Greece."

On his deathbed Partap made his successor swear to eternal conflict against "the foes of his country's independence." This was in the sixteenth century, four hundred years after the first Muslim king had ascended the throne of Delhi. But a hundred years had hardly gone by after the event when the Hindus again questioned Muslim supremacy. The Sikhs in the Punjab, the Rajputs in Central India, and the Mahrattas in the Deccan, had started their campaigns before Aurangzeb died in 1707 A. D. The Muslim supremacy was destroyed by the Hindus and not by the British.

Muslim Rule in India not Foreign. Yet it is not right to say that the Muslim rule in India was a "foreign rule." The Muslim invaders were no doubt foreign in their origin, just as the Normans and Danes were when they came to England, but as soon as they settled in India, adopted the country, made it their home, married and raised children there, they became the sons of the soil. Akbar and Aurangzeb were as much Indians as are to-day the Moguls and Pathans in Delhi or elsewhere. Sher Shah and Ibrahim Lodi were no more foreigners in

India than were the descendants of William the Conqueror or the successors of William of Orange in Great Britain. When Timur and Nadir Shah and Ahmad Shah Abdali attacked India, they attacked a kingdom which was ruled by Indian Muslims. They were as much the enemies of the Mohammedan rulers of India as of the Hindus.

The Muslims, who exercised political sovereignty in India from the thirteenth up to the middle of the nineteenth century A. D., were Indians by birth, Indians by marriage, and Indians by death. They were born in India, they married there, there they died, and there they were buried. Every penny of the revenues they raised in India was spent in India. Their army was wholly Indian. They allowed new families from beyond the borders of Hindustan to come and settle in India, but they very rarely, if at all, employed people who were not willing to stay in India for good and to make it their home. Their bias, if any, against the Hindus was religious, not political. The converts to Islam were sometimes treated even with greater consideration than the original Muslims. Akbar, of course, did away with that distinction, but even the most bigoted and the most orthodox Mohammedan ruler of India was not possessed of that kind of social pride and social exclusiveness which distinguishes the British ruler of India to-day. If the racial question ever came into prominence during Mohammedan supremacy in India, it was not between Hindus and Mohammedans, but between Mohammedans and

Mohammedans, as for instance between *Tuglaks* and *Pathans,* or between *Moguls* and *Lodis.*[8]

In the reign of rulers like Sher Shah, Akbar, Jehangir, and Shah Jahan, the Hindus were eligible for the highest offices under the crown next after the princes of royal blood. They were governors of provinces, generals of armies, and rulers of districts and divisions. In short, the distinctions between the Hindus and Muslims were neither political nor social. Looked at from the political and the economic point of view, the Government was as much indigenous as under Hindu rule. The Muslims never attempted to disarm the population; nor did they prohibit the manufacture or import of arms. They did not recruit their servants from Arabia, or Persia, or Afghanistan. They had no Lancashire industries to protect, and were under no necessity of imposing excise duties on Indian-made goods. They brought their own language and literature with them. For a time, perhaps, they transacted all government business through that language, but eventually they evolved a language which is as much Indian as any other vernacular spoken in India to-day. The groundwork of this language, which is now called Urdu or Hindustani, is purely Indian. The Muslim rulers of India had no anxiety for, and were in no way concerned with, the prosperity of the labouring classes of Persia or Afghanistan. If any one sought their patronage, he had to come to and settle in India. So their

[8] The history of Europe up to the 18th century is full of parallel disputes on racial and religious grounds.

government was an Indian government and not a foreign government.

History does not record a single instance of India being ruled from without, by a people of purely non-Indian blood and in the interests of another country and another people, before the British.[9] India was always an empire by herself. She was never a part of another empire, much less a dependency. She had her own army, her own navy, her own flag. Her revenues were spent for her own benefit. She had her industries and manufactured the goods she consumed. Any one wanting the privilege of trading with India under special terms had to obtain the sanction of her government, as the East India Company did. There was no India Office in Arabia or in Persia or in Kabul, to which the people of India looked for initiative in the affairs of their native land.

INDIA UNDER THE BRITISH

India under the British is, however, entirely different.[10] For the first time in history she becomes

[9] It is said that for a short time a small portion of Northwest India formed a province of the Empire of Darius and paid tribute to that monarch, but the government was all the same native.

[10] "The Asiatic conquerors very soon abated their ferocity, because they made the conquered country their own. They rose or fell with the rise and fall of the territory they lived in. Fathers there deposited the hopes of their posterity; the children there beheld the monuments of their fathers. Here their lot was finally cast; and it is the normal wish of all that their lot should not be cast in bad land. Poverty, sterility, and desolation are not a recreating prospect to the eye of man, and there are very few who can bear to grow old among the curses of a whole people. If their passion or avarice drove the Tar-

a part of another empire. India to-day is not an empire by herself, but a part of the British Empire, as Britain once was a part of the Roman Empire. For the first time in history she has been reduced to the position of a dependency. For the first time in her history she is ruled from the outside. For the first time the Indians have been reduced to the

tar hordes to acts of rapacity or tyranny, there was time enough, even in the short life of man, to bring round the ill effects of the abuse of power upon the power itself. If hoards were made by violence and tyranny, they were still domestic hoards, and domestic profusion, or the rapine of a more powerful and prodigal hand, restored them to the people. With many disorders and with few political checks upon power, nature had still fair play, the sources of acquisition were not dried up, and therefore the trade, the manufactures, and the commerce of the country flourished. Even avarice and usury itself operated both for the preservation and the employment of national wealth. The husbandman and manufacturer paid heavy interest, but then they augmented the fund from whence they were again to borrow. Their resources were dearly bought, but they were sure, and the general stock of the community grew by the general effect.

"But under the English Government all this order is reversed. The Tartar invasion was mischievous, but it is our protection that destroys India. It was their enmity, but it is our friendship. Our conquest there, after twenty years, is as crude as it was the first day. The natives scarcely know what it is to see the grey head of an Englishman; young men, boys almost, govern there, without society, and without sympathy with the natives. They have no more social habits with the people than if they still resided in England; nor, indeed, any species of intercourse but that which is necessary to making a sudden fortune, with a view to a remote settlement. Animated with all the avarice of age, and all the impetuosity of youth, they roll in one after another, wave after wave, and there is nothing before the eyes of the natives but an endless, hopeless prospect of new flights of birds of prey and passage, with appetites continually renewing for a food that is continually wasting. Every rupee of profit made by an Englishman is lost forever to India." (Edmund Burke in a speech made in the House of Commons in 1783 A. D. The reflections are as good, to-day, as they were then.)

position of a subject people, governed by an alien race residing in a different and far-off country. For the first time she is ruled by a sovereign who does not live in India, who sends out every five years a viceroy to administer the affairs of the country under the authority of a minister in a foreign land. For the first time her affairs are managed by people who come and go, under laws made outside of India.[11] All the chief offices of state, the direction and control of armies, the administration of revenues, of divisions, of districts, the coining of money, the administration of justice, the imposing of taxes, etc., are generally in the hands of foreigners who have absolutely no interest in the country except as servants of the crown, persons whose interests in the country cease with the expiration of their term of service. These servants are recruited and appointed out of India. Indians as such are virtually ineligible for many of these offices. During the 150 years of British rule in India, no Indian has been appointed to the governorship of any province. Indians are ineligible for commissions in the army; they cannot be enrolled as volunteers. In order to qualify for the Civil service of their own country, they have to travel six thousand miles, to take the chance of succeeding once in a while.

Political Disqualification of the Indians. For the first time in the political history of India it has become a political disqualification to be an

[11] The constitution of the Government of India is settled by laws made by the Parliament of Great Britain, in which India is not represented.

Indian. The offspring of an Englishman, domiciled in India and married to an Indian lady, loses in rank and status by that fact; nor does the issue of an Indian gentleman from an Englishwoman gain anything thereby. So the inferiority in both ways lies in Indian blood and Indian origin. The Muslim who married in India, or the Indian who married a Persian or Afghan, were not affected thereby in their political privileges in the Mohammedan régime. An Indian convert to Christianity is in no better position in India than a Hindu or a Muslim. Thus it is not a religious inferiority or a religious distinction, upon which the political disabilities of an Indian are based, but the fact of his being an Indian by blood and by birth. Never before was India governed by a handful of officers, military and civil, who came to rule for a period, going away when that period was over, only to be replaced by another set equally temporary. India thus loses all or most of what these receive in the shape of money; she loses all the experience which they gain in the different spheres of activity that engages them during the period of their service in India; last but not least, she is deprived of the satisfaction and pride of claiming these men as her sons, who would in their turn take pride in her and feel as sons should for their mother. They come as her rulers, and till the end remain the same. Their sons and grandsons also may in their turn come as rulers, but never as sons. The sons of India, who gain the rank of officials, are only servants of the British. Their position in the Indian services is generally that of drawers of water and hewers of wood for their British masters.

All Europeans, Eurasians including Armenians and Jews can carry arms free of license; not so the Indians. In India, the Indians only are forbidden to carry arms except by special permission of their masters; and permission is of course granted very sparingly and as a matter of favour, as a special concession and not as a right. The highest, the noblest, and the purest among the Indians has to be *excepted* from the operation of the Arms Act, as an act of mercy on the part of his foreign rulers. In the hills of his own native country, where his parents, grandparents, and great grandparents before him were born, where they perhaps ruled or held positions of trust, where they died, where they fertilised the soil with their blood, and where within less than a century they enjoyed absolute freedom, he, their immediate descendant, must not carry an umbrella over his head to give him shelter from rain or sun without the risk of being kicked to death or being insulted by the lowest among the foreign masters of his country.[12] The hoary Himalayas, the beloved abode of his most respected divinities, are in some places virtually shut against him because the "white gods" have developed a fancy for them.

But that is not all. Even outside India he carries the badge of political subjection with him. The British colonies, more than any other country, bang their doors on him. He is a pariah all over

[12] See Sir Henry Cotton's New India (1907), pp. 68, 69 and 70.

the world. Considering that this is his position in his home, he could hardly be anything else outside. The British Government does not like his going abroad except as an indentured coolie to the British colonies. He may go to England on a pleasure trip, but they do not want Indians there in any numbers. They particularly dislike his going to America and settling there. The reason is obvious. Travelling abroad gives him opportunities of comparing British rule in India with the forms of government prevailing in other countries. Free atmosphere and free environment raise aspirations which are dangerous, at any rate inconvenient to British supremacy in India. Moreover, they effectively break down the hypnotism which has so far enthralled the Indian mind in its judgments regarding British character. On his return to India, a travelled Indian becomes a centre of discontent. In the course of their travels some Indians meet the free-thinkers and revolutionaries of Europe and learn their methods. All this is naturally disliked by the British.

Therefore, of late, the British have been taking steps to discourage foreign travelling on the part of Indians. They have been trying to keep Indian students out of Great Britain by imposing conditions which are repellent. They have raised the educational standards which had formerly secured them admission into British universities and British Inns of Court. They have organised an official bureau in London which, ostensibly acting as their guardian and adviser, discourages them from entering British universities, keeps a vigilant eye on their movements, reports on their conduct to the authorities at home, and insists upon their seeking admission to British educational institutions through it.[13] At all Indian ports there are police officers present, who note down the names of, and particulars relating to, every Indian who leaves Indian shores. Thenceforth two eyes are almost always watching him, go wherever he may.

To him, the British embassies in the different countries of the world mean nothing. He is afraid of seeking their help, first for fear of getting a rebuff and being insulted, second because he is afraid of circumstances being created which might force his early departure from that country. His wrongs are nobody's wrongs. He may be assaulted, nay, even killed, or insulted, or robbed, or ill-treated, yet he has no government to look to his interests. The British Government does not resent other countries' excluding him; they are rather happy at it and in some cases are understood to have exercised their influence against his entry into foreign countries. The self-governing dominions of the British Empire have built a solid wall of most revolting and inhuman laws and regulations against his entry into those dominions. He cannot go there, even on a pleasure trip or for study, except by submitting to impossible tests or most revolting conditions.

[13] In England this is the view of the bulk of the Indian student community. The Government, of course, repudiates that view.

In this respect he is much better treated by non-British countries. Till recently he could come and go there quite freely. No European country bars his visits. Of late the United States, it is said, at the instance of the British Government, has been following a policy of exclusion. But once in the country, all universities and institutions receive him, provided he fulfils their conditions and complies with their regulations. That much, however, cannot be said of Great Britain. It is true that Great Britain imposes no restrictions on his coming and going, as she imposes no restrictions on any one else's coming and going, but there are British institutions which would not admit him as a student, however high his social position or status may be. Even those institutions which admit him for study, discriminate against him in the matter of military drill. They would not admit him into their volunteer corps; nor would they take him as a boy scout. A great many of the British clubs would have nothing to do with him. The only British club of note, which has a fairly good number of Indians on its rolls and which accords them a welcome, is the National Liberal Club. This club is a noble exception.

Now the British must be an extremely unimaginative people, if they think that all this does not make the Indian feel the inferiority of his position. The latter, naturally, ascribes all this to the fact of his country's having no national government of her own to protect him and to advance his interests. All this reminds him most forcibly of the fact that he belongs to a subject race, that his country does not count in the world because she is not free and has no embassies, that she has no flag of her own, nor consular representatives to back her sons, and that in the great mass of civilised humanity he is a mere cypher. All this naturally tells on his nerves and he becomes an extremist. He feels that anything would be preferable to this life of shame and dishonor.

It is difficult for people who have never been placed in a similar position to realise the sense of humiliation and shame involved in this condition of things. Let the British for a moment imagine themselves under similar circumstances, and they may then be in a position to appreciate the point of view of an Indian nationalist. Let us suppose for a moment that the Germans conquer England and impose their rule on the British race. How would the British like their country being administered by a viceroy of the Kaiser selected by the German Chancellor, with the help of a council consisting of Germans and of a bureaucracy recruited almost exclusively from Prussia, with only a sprinkling of native Britishers? No one can question the efficiency of the German system. The strong hand of Germany might keep Ireland in peace and prevent the suffragists and the socialists and the Roman Catholics disturbing public tranquillity. They might even employ a whole army of Britishers in the subordinate posts, might pay them handsomely for military and police duty, might confer decorations and titles on them, might build even greater engineering works for them than they had ever done, and might let them retain their language for elementary education or for religious or domestic purposes. Would the English be satisfied and would they be contented? Would they consider German rule to be a blessing and judge it by trade returns? Never![13a] Why then, should they question the patriotism or good sense of the Indians who want self-government for India? Did not Sir Henry Campbell-Bannerman say that good government could never be a substitute for self-government?

The fact is, that it is impossible for a free-born citizen of a free country to put himself in the position of a political subject and realise fully and properly the sense of humiliation and shame involved therein. The feeling is unknown to him, and he has not sufficient imagination to place himself in that position. Why cannot a Britisher see that every Indian, visiting foreign countries, has to hang his head in shame?

British statesmen, politicians, publicists and journalists all talk of the blessings of British rule in India, of what the British have done there in establishing peace and order, in making railways and canals, in imparting education, in stimulating trade, in administering impartial justice, in fostering in-

[13a] In this connection we may refer the reader to an excellent article published in the *New Statesman* (London) dated April 1, 1916, called, "If the Germans conquered England." With the alteration of England for Germany and India for England the article would make an excellent exposition of the position of the Indian Nationalist.

dustries, in organising the postal and the telegraph systems, and in opening the country to the world. They cannot see why the Indian should wish to get rid of the British. The British have done so much for him, have brought civilisation to his door, have raised him from "obscurity," have given him their language and their institutions, have opened to him the gates of knowledge, have provided for him security from both domestic and foreign dangers, and have put him on the road to ever-increasing prosperity and *"happiness."* Let us assume for the moment that all this is wholly true, but can it compensate for the loss of manhood which is involved in political bondage? Chains are chains, no matter if gilded. Can the wealth of the whole world be put in the scales over against liberty and honour? What would it avail if one were to get the sovereignty of the world but lose his own soul? A subject people has no soul, just as a slave can have none. Subjects and slaves are not even the masters of their bodies.

An Indian leader, a high-class Bengali lawyer, who is now one of His Majesty's judges in the High Court of Calcutta, once said, while presiding over a conference in Bengal before he became a judge, that a subject people could have no politics. A people who have no politics have no soul. A man without a soul is a mere animal. A nation without a soul is only a herd of "dumb driven cattle," and such are the Indians of the present day. It is a base calumny, and a mean falsehood to say in reply, that they have been so from time immemorial, that they have never been free, that they have never cared who ruled over them, that they have never been patriotic, or that patriotism and a feeling of nationality are new growths due to contact with the West, and that the Indian people do not sympathise with the aspirations of the nationalists. Of course, there are some people in India, as elsewhere, who, through rolling in wealth, living in purple, inheriting long pedigrees, carrying high titles, bearing proud names, seem to be happy and contented under the existing conditions. For them, the security from molestation they have, the freedom of enjoyment they possess, the comforts and luxuries which they command, the pleasure which is born of inactive, lazy, parasitic, debauched lives, is all in all. Any change may bring all this edifice down; it may spell ruin to them and their children. The immunity from work, which they at present enjoy, may all disappear by a change of political conditions. The British Government has guaranteed them not only their possessions, but also their right to live and thrive on the ignorance, the superstitions, and the mental and moral slavery of their followers and subjects.

Such are some of the Nabobs and Maharajas of India. Many of them might have to cut stones and make roads to earn their living, if they were not protected by British bayonets. Their harems consisting of numerous innocent women doomed to life-long imprisonment, to lives of barrenness and shame and emptiness, their big cellars full of the choicest and the oldest of whiskies, brandies, and champagnes, their stables full of the swiftest and the noblest of race horses, their drawing rooms decorated with gold, silver, silk and velvet, all that money can buy and art can embellish, their dining tables laden with all inviting dishes and delicacies which the best paid *cuisine* in the world can produce, their ability to travel in special trains and gorgeous saloons, and to command a new woman and a new wine every day of the year, and to move in the most fashionable circles,—all depend on the continuance of the existing conditions. For them, this is life. They do not know what honour is. For them, struggle, strife, duty, political change, mean a dislocation of everything dear to them. It would be practical death to them. Yes, it may be true that such people do not care for political liberty, for freedom, for independence, for patriotism. For them, their present life is bliss and they do not want to be molested either by the politician or by the patriot.

But their number is not large. Some of the ruling chiefs may not speak out, but in their heart of hearts many of them feel the humiliation of the situation. A Maharana of Udeypore may not be in a position to assert his independence and take the chance of losing his State, but even *he* may not consent to walk behind a Curzon in a coronation procession in honour of the King of England and the foreign Emperor of India. A Gaekwar of Baroda may be powerless as against the British army and British navy, but even he, in a moment of exalted self-respect, may forget to make an abject obeisance to the King of England. Such men and even many of less worth and nobility, cannot put up with a Lord Curzon. It is good for their sense of self-respect and also for the country at large to have a Curzon for a viceroy. It reminds them, as nothing else perhaps would, of their degradation and fall.

It is very interesting to observe how the Indian Chiefs writhe and fret and foam when a Curzon threatens their privileges, tries to limit their freedom, and otherwise trespasses upon their rights. It is then that a wave of shame sweeps over them and touches some lingering sense of self-respect and pride in their hearts. But the infamous, lazy, debauched lives which some of them have led make it impossible for them to maintain this indignation long enough for it to goad them to any sustained effort to throw away their thraldom and assert their manhood. The injecting of an electric current may temporarily revive a dead body, may produce some kind of activity even in a parasite, but it cannot put *life* into it.

But after all, as compared with the number of people who are alive to the sense of self-respect and honour, the parasitical crowned heads or priests or noblemen (Nabobs, Rajas, and Maharajas) are only a few. They are a mere drop in the ocean, though they possess the means of keeping themselves in the public eye and of having their trumpets blown and praises sung by the press and from the platform both in India and in England. The British too are interested in keeping them at the front, in parading their loyalty and devotion to the empire, and in magnifying their importance and greatness.

There are few among the nobility of India who command any real respect either from the educated section of their countrymen in general, or even from their own subjects and dependents. Of course there are noble exceptions to this statement. And yet it is true that a large number of ruling chiefs are mere figureheads in their states. Their policy is either dictated or guided or controlled by the British Resident or the British Political Agent through his creatures or through persons, who, though not quite his creatures, are afraid of his displeasure. In some states, the Resident interferes in almost everything, and all the details of administration pass through his fingers either directly or indirectly. In others, the Resident watches the administration from a distance and lays down the broad outlines of policy. There are few native states, their number may be counted on one's fingers, where the ruling chief has a will or capacity to really assert himself, to stand on his dignity, and to maintain his independence. Even the most enlightened and the most independent Prince is compelled to consult the wishes of the Resident and the wishes of the Government of India as expressed by him.

Loyalty of Ruling Chiefs. It would be quite wrong to conclude, as some people do, that all the ruling chiefs are sincerely loyal to the British supremacy, or that their acts displaying loyalty are free and independent expressions of their minds or their will.[14] Some of them are devoid of any real sense of honour, or are lost to it by habitual submission or habitual debauchery. They are quite contented to be left alone to enjoy. There are others, however, who would be only too glad to throw away the British yoke, if they could only see a way of successfully doing so. They are not prepared to take their chances. It should be distinctly understood, therefore, that the Nationalist Party does not count upon their help or sympathy. A good many perhaps sympathise with the party of violence, and chuckle at their successes, but none of them dare do anything to help them in any shape. A few openly sympathise with the "constitutional" party, but even they cannot and would not give them any monetary or other kind of help as it might easily be construed into an act of unfriendliness towards the Paramount Power, and might mar their relations with that.

The smaller fry, the wealthy banker, the great landlord, the Bengal Zemindar, and the Oudh Talukdar, are almost completely in the hands of the British officials. The sympathy of the British officials benefits them materially. Their antipathy or dislike or aversion would ruin them financially. The British collector or magistrate holds complete sway over their souls. They would rather go out of their way to propitiate him and win his pleasure, than risk the slightest suspicion of an independent attitude, or of any conduct which even by stretch of imagination could be construed into independ-

[14] See New India by Sir Henry Cotton, 1907, p. 34.

ence. Yet there are some, in Bengal at least, who do sympathise with, and give active help to, the Revolutionary Party. There are others who sympathise with, and give occasional monetary assistance to, the Constitutional Party. The latter class does not count for much in Indian politics, and anything said or done by them cannot be said to represent the attitude of any very large section of the Indian community.

Men of wealth and men of means have nowhere led the revolutionary or the political movements in the history of freedom in this world of ours. Their interests as a class are opposed to change. Sometimes there does arise from among their ranks a man of courage, a man endowed with an adventurous nature or fired by ambition, who leads the movement for change, in the hope of either establishing a dynasty, or otherwise leaving a name in history; and sometimes one comes across a wealthy man who, out of regard for principle, and from conviction, is a patriot, and joins the patriotic party deliberately, and risks his possessions and position; but such instances are always few and far between in all countries.

Middle Class Desires Political Freedom. The desire for political independence, the sense of shame and humiliation born of being a subject race, of being a political pariah, must from the nature of things be confined largely to the educated middle class. Even the masses could not be expected to take a very deep interest in the movement for political independence. Their ignorance, their illiteracy, but most of all the hard struggle they have to carry on for barest existence, prevents them from devoting time or thought to the question. Their time and thought are given to the fight against hunger and want, against disease and distress, against misery and wretchedness. They are easy to please. A slight act of kindness or of charity or of consideration makes them happy. They are easily confused on fundamental issues. This is true even in Europe and America, where the common people have received the benefits of school education, and where they have had a training in democratic thought for a century or more. The masses are easily led astray by governments or by classes in league with governments. In every country it is the educated middle class that leads the movement for political independence or for political progress. It is the strength of their convictions, their earnestness, their capacity to suffer for their convictions, their willingness to sacrifice themselves for principles and for truth, coupled with the extent and amount of their influence over the masses, which determines the fate of the movement for liberty.

A movement of that nature never dies. "The battle of freedom once begun is carried on from father to son," is as good to-day as it ever was. Yet the movement may be delayed, or its issue may be confused, or the contrary, according to the wisdom or the folly of its advocates, or the amount of earnestness they put in it, or the amount of influence they have over the masses, as well as by the wisdom or shortsightedness or cunning of those who oppose it. All the world over, progressive political movements have had vicissitudes of fortune, stages of development, times of reactions, defeats and reverses. Governments always begin by ignoring such movements. Then comes a period of ridicule, followed by repression. But their efforts are futile. The food on which the tender plant of liberty thrives is the blood of the martyr. The rope of the hangman, the axe of the executioner, or the shot of the gunner, extinguishes individual life, only to make the desire for corporate life keener and stronger. Banishments, deportations, imprisonments, tortures and confiscations, are the usual weapons of the tyrant to strangle liberty, to extirpate those that are after it, but they have so far proved ineffectual to kill it. Conciliation is sometimes more successful than repression, but conciliation delayed or concessions forced have been proved to be worse than useless. The Nationalist Movement in India has passed through some of these stages, and is passing through the rest. We presume it will be of some interest and use to trace its development, and to make a retrospective review of its successes and failures so far.[15]

[15] It should be noted that the evils complained of in this chapter are the evils of the system which, in the words of John Stuart Mill, is unnatural, and the unnaturalness of which is recognised in full by many fair-minded Britishers. It was recognised so far back as 1835 by the British historian Wilson in his concluding remarks in the last chapter of his monumental History of British India.

CHAPTER II

INDIA FROM 1757 TO 1857 A. D.

AURANGZEB, the 6th Mogul Emperor of India, died in 1707 A. D. Within fifty years of his death, the Mogul sovereignty in India was reduced to its last gasp. The seeds sown by his bigotry, fanaticism, and suspicious nature were ripening and bringing to his successors a harvest of dissensions and discords, of rebellions and revolts. In the North as well as the South, forces had been generated which threatened the end of the Mogul rule. The martyrdom of Guru Teg Bahadur, the Sikh Guru, who was foully murdered at Delhi, where he had gone on a mission of peace, had sunk deep into the hearts of his followers, and his son, Guru Govind Singh, was organising forces which were destined to supplant Mogul rule in the Land of the Five Rivers.[1] In the Deccan, Sivaji's[2] standard and throne had become the rallying point of the fighting forces of Southern India.

By 1757 A. D., the Sikhs in the Punjab and the Mahrattas in the Deccan had succeeded in undermining the foundations of the Mogul rule, which was now steadily disintegrating. The Nizam of Hyderabad, and the Nawab of Mysore had asserted

[1] The Punjab.
[2] Sivaji was the founder of the Mahratta Empire in India.

their independence and were disputing the mastery of the Deccan with the Mahrattas. Similarly the Nabobs of Bengal and Oudh owed only nominal allegiance to the King of Delhi. The greater part of the peninsula, Central India, was under the Mahrattas.

Conflict of French and English in India. The political fate of India was hanging in the balance, when a power arose to take advantage of the disturbed conditions of things. The French and the English both entered the arena, taking different sides, and began to shuffle their cards. They sold their help to the highest bidder, and at the conclusion of every game, or even in the midst of it, changed partners as often as they could in the interest of their respective masters. The first military achievement of note, which gave decisive advantage to the British, was at the battle of Plassey in 1757. That practically gave them the key to the sovereignty of India. From 1757 to 1857 was the century of struggle, both military and diplomatic. The one end kept in view was the making of the Empire and the amassing of wealth.

How British Rule in India was Established. Hindus were played against the Mohammedans, and vice versa, states and principalities against states and principalities, Jats against Rajputs, and Rajputs against Jats, Mahrattas against both, Rohillas against Bundelas, and Bundelas against Pathans, and so on. Treaties were made and broken without the least scruple, sides were taken and changed and again changed without the least consideration of honour or faith. Thrones were purchased and sold to the highest bidder. Military support was purchased and given like merchandise. Servants were induced to betray their masters, soldiers to desert flags, without any regard to the morality of the steps taken. Pretences were invented and occasions sought for involving states and principalities in wars and trouble. Laws of all kinds, national and international, moral and religious, were all for the time thrown into the discard. Neither minors nor widows received any consideration; the young and the old were treated alike. The one object in view was to loot, to plunder, and to make an empire. Everything was subordinated to that end. One has only to read Mill and Wilson's "History of British India," Burke's "Impeachment of Warren Hastings," Torrens' "Our Empire in Asia," Wilson's "Sword and Ledger," Bell's "Annexation of the Punjab" to find out that the above is a bare and moderate statement of truth.

Methods of Consolidation of British India. Policies (fiscal, industrial, religious, educational) were all discussed and formulated from one point of view, viz., the establishing of British authority, the consolidation of British rule, and pecuniary gain to the East India Company. If one were to pile up "scraps of paper" which the British destroyed or disregarded in the making of their Indian empire, one could fill a decent sized box therewith. The administrations of Wellesley and Dalhousie alone would furnish sufficient material for the purpose. We do not know of anything in Indian history which could be compared with the deeds of this century. It was a century of consistent, prolonged, and deliberate spoliation, subtle and scientific sometimes, in the pursuance of which all laws of morality, humanity, and fairness were tossed aside, and the object in view was persistently and doggedly kept in view and achieved. It was not the doing of this man or that man, but, with some noble exceptions, of the whole body of Administrators sent by the East India Company to manage their affairs in the East. The policies and doings of the various rulers that were sent from England to administer the affairs of India differed in degree only.

British Public Ignorant of Facts. It is true that the British people as a whole had no notion of what was going on in India. They were as ignorant of it, then, as they are to-day of the doings of their countrymen in that vast "continent." It sufficed for them to know that their countrymen were carving an empire there, conquering provinces and bringing millions of alien people under British rule; as it suffices for them to know to-day that they have an empire in India. India brought them wealth and material prosperity. Individuals became fabulously rich and their wealth filtered downward and filled the whole British nation. The nation became rich by the dividends of the East India Company, and by the enormous profits which British manufacturers and British traders made by the fact of British supremacy in

India. That was enough for the nation. Even when their moral sense was at times shocked by certain disclosures, which by chance found their way into the press or into the literature of the country, it was soon calmed and set at rest by the speeches made by the statesmen at the helm of affairs, who explained them away, excused their authors on political grounds, and laid down in high, grandiloquent terms that the general aim of British rule in India was beneficent, and that this aim was steadily being pursued. The impeachment of Warren Hastings by Burke should have opened the eyes of the British public as to what was happening in India; but the eventual acquittal of that famous pro-consul set matters at rest. And Warren Hastings was by no means the worst offender. What happened then is happening every day in India, only in a different way and on a different scale.

Yet I am not disposed to criticise the British public. Democracies have no time for the critical examination of the affairs of other countries and other people. They have their own trouble, enough and to spare. They look to material benefits, and their imagination is fired and their mind is thrilled by the fact of so many millions being under their rule. In the case of the British, both combined make them proud of their countrymen, who rule and administer India in their name. They have no reason to be critical. Human nature is human nature after all. Ordinary human nature is not inclined to be critical at gains, especially when it does not directly feel the iniquity of the methods by which those gains are made. But this is only by the way.

To continue the thread of my narrative: the history of British "conquest" of India from 1757 to 1857 A. D. is a continuous record of political charlatanry, political faithlessness, and political immorality. It was a triumph of British "diplomacy." The British founders of the Indian empire had the true imperial instincts of empire-builders. They cared little for the means which they employed. Moral theorists cannot make empires. Empires can only be built by unscrupulous men of genius, men of daring and dash, making the best of opportunities that come to their hands, caring little for the wrongs which they thereby inflict on others, or the dishonesties or treacheries or breaches of faith involved therein. Empires can only be conceived by Napoleons, Bismarcks, Disraelis, Richelieus, and Machiavellis. They can only be built by Clives, Hastings, Wellesleys, and Dalhousies. Burkes and Gladstones cannot do that work, nor can Morleys, though they may connive at others doing it, and might accept it as *fait accompli*.

Conquest of India Diplomatic, not Military. The British conquest of India was not a military conquest in any sense of the term. They could not conquer India except by playing on the fears of some and the hopes of others, and by seeking and getting the help of Indians, both moral and material. The record is as black as it could be; but nothing succeeds like success, and all that is largely a forgotten page so far as the present generation of Indians is concerned. Only one feels disposed to smile when one hears of Indian nationalists being charged in British-Indian courts with attempting to subvert "the government established by law." One is inclined to ask "By what law?" and "Who made that law?"

The Great Indian Mutiny of 1857. We have, however, referred to this story in these few words only to introduce the great Indian mutiny of 1857, as the first Indian political movement of the nineteenth century. *The movement was national as well as political. The underlying causes and the contributory forces were many.* The union of the Hindus and Mohammedans, the thoroughness of the organisation which preceded the mutiny, the stubbornness with which the mutineers fought, and the comparatively few treacheries that characterised the mutinous campaign, all point to the same conclusion.

The mutiny, however, failed because the people on the whole had no faith in the constructive capacity of the mutineers. The mutineers had no doubt agreed to postpone the question of the constructive ends in view, until after they had turned out the British, but the people could not. The people's patience had been exhausted by the military activities of the preceding century and the accompanying disorder and anarchy, and they saw before them the possibility of a recurrence of the same in the case of success attending the arms of the mutineers. They hated the British; the Indian nobility and aristocracy, as well as the Indian people, hated them. They sympathised with the mutineers; but they helped them only half-heartedly. They had no faith in them. The ruling families of India, the aristocracy and the nobility, were perhaps more dreaded and hated by the people than were the British. There was no one to rally them to one standard.

How the Mutiny was Put Down. Here again it was British "diplomacy" that saved the British situation. The British rallied to their support the newly born aristocracy of the Punjab,—the Sikhs. The Sikhs had been persecuted and oppressed by the Mohammedans. They were not in a mood to look favourably at the chance of Mohammedan supremacy being re-established in India. They had had enough of the "Turk," as they called every Mohammedan; and they threw the whole weight of their recently gathered virility on the side of the British. They were told and they believed, that in crushing the Mohammedan power, they were revenging themselves on the slayers of Guru Teg Bahadur, the oppressors of Guru Govind Singh, and the murderers of his sons. It was the thought of Sirhind and the incidents associated with the name of that cursed place,[3] that goaded them to the destruction of the last chance of Mohammedan supremacy in India.

The mutiny failed, but its course showed with what intensity the mutineers hated the British. The

[3] Sirhind is a small town on the road to Delhi, where the Muslim governor of the time tortured the two minor sons of Guru Govind Singh to death by placing them between two brick walls.

Indians are a very kind-hearted people; they would not injure even an ant, much less a human being, if they could help it, but some of them were guilty of the most cruel excesses during the mutiny. The British, too, in their turn did not spare the Indians in any way either during the mutiny or after it. Innocent and guilty alike were placed before the cannon and shot in lots.[4] In their marches through the country, British soldiers tortured men, women, and children,[5] and sometimes hung their heads or

[4] See Kaye and Malleson, vol. II, p. 367. "In respect to the mutineers of the 55th, they were taken fighting against us, and so far deserve little mercy. But, on full reflection, I would not put them all to death. I do not think that we should be justified in the eyes of the Almighty in doing so. A hundred and twenty men are a large number to put to death. Our object is to make an example to terrify others. I think this object would be effectually gained by destroying from a quarter to a third of them. I would select all of those against whom anything bad can be shown — such as general bad character, turbulence, prominence in disaffection or in the fight, disrespectful demeanor to their officers during the few days before the 26th, and the like. If these did not make up the required number, I would then add to them the oldest soldiers. All these should be shot or blown away from the guns, as may be most expedient. The rest I would divide into patches: some to be imprisoned ten years, some seven, some five, some three."

[5] History of Indian Mutiny, Kaye and Malleson, vol. II, p. 203. "Martial law had been proclaimed; those terrible Acts passed by the Legislative Council in May and June were in full operation; and soldiers and civilians alike were holding Bloody Assize, or slaying natives without any Assize at all, regardless of sex or age. Afterwards the thirst for blood grew stronger still. It is on the records of our British Parliament, in papers sent home by the Governor General of India in Council, that the aged, women, and children, are sacrificed, as well as those guilty of rebellion. They were not deliberately hanged, but burnt to death in their villages — perhaps now and then accidently shot. Englishmen did not hesitate to boast, or to record their boastings in writings, that they had 'spared no one,' and that 'peppering away at niggers' was very pleasant pastime, 'enjoyed amazingly.' It has been stated in a book

carcasses on the trees.[6] Both sides vied with each other in their cruelties.

The victors have immortalised the reprisals (or say, the iniquities) of the vanquished by building

patronised by high class authorities, that 'for three months eight dead-carts daily went their rounds from sunrise to sunset to take down the corpses which hung at the cross-roads and market-places,' and that 'six thousand beings' had been thus summarily disposed of and launched into eternity."

[6] See Kaye and Malleson's History of the Mutiny, vol. II, p. 177. "Already our military officers were hunting down the criminals of all kinds, and hanging them up with as little compunction as though they had been pariah-dogs, or jackals, or vermin of a baser kind. One contemporary writer has recorded that, on the morning of disarming parade, the first thing he saw from the Mint was a 'row of gallowses.' A few days afterwards the military courts or commissions were sitting daily, and sentencing old and young to be hanged with indiscriminate ferocity. On one occasion, some young boys, who, seemingly in mere sport, had flaunted rebel colours and gone about beating tom-toms, were tried and sentenced to death. One of the officers composing the court, a man unsparing before an enemy under arms, but compassionate, as all brave men are, towards the weak and the helpless, went with tears in his eyes to the commanding officer, imploring him to remit the sentence passed against these juvenile offenders, but with little effect on the side of mercy. And what was done with some show of formality either of military or of criminal law, was as nothing, I fear, weighed against what was done without any formality at all. Volunteer hanging parties went out into the districts, and amateur executioners were not wanting to the occasion. One gentleman boasted of the numbers he had finished off quite 'in an artistic manner,' with mango-trees for gibbets and elephants for drops, the victims of this wild justice being strung up, as though for pastime, in 'the form of a figure of eight.'"

On mock trials see Holmes' History of the Sepoy War, p. 124. "Officers, as they went to sit on the court martial, swore that they would hang their prisoners, guilty or innocent. . . . Prisoners condemned to death after a hasty trial were mocked at and tortured by ignorant privates before their execution, while educated officers looked on and approved." "Old men who had done us no harm, and helpless women with sucking infants at their breasts felt the weight of our vengeance, no less than the vilest malefactors."

permanent memorials on the spots where they were perpetrated; their own, they have forgotten, and so have perhaps the descendants of those who were the objects thereof, though they are recorded in history.

Again see History of the Siege of Delhi quoted by Savarkar in his "War of Indian Independence," p. 111, by an officer who served there, how, on the way from Umbala to Delhi, thousands were placed before a court martial in rows after rows and condemned to be hanged or shot. In some places cow's flesh was forced by spears and bayonets into the mouths of the condemned. (All Hindus abhor cow's flesh and would rather die than eat it.)

See Charles Ball's Indian Mutiny, vol. I, p. 257. "One trip I enjoyed amazingly; we got on board a steamer with a gun, while the Sikhs and the fusiliers marched up to the city. We steamed up throwing shots right and left till we got up to the bad places, when we went on the shore and peppered away with our guns, my old double-barrel bringing down several niggers. So thirsty for vengeance I was. We fired the places right and left and the flames shot up to the heavens as they spread, fanned by the breeze, showing that the day of vengeance had fallen on the treacherous villains. Every day we had expeditions to burn and destroy disaffected villages and we had taken our revenge. I have been appointed the chief of a commission for the trial of all natives charged with offences against the Government and persons. Day by day, we have strung up eight or ten men. We have the power of life in our hands and, I assure you, we spare not. A very summary trial is all that takes place. The condemned culprit is placed under a tree, with a rope around his neck, on the top of a carriage, and when it is pulled off he swings."

"In the Punjab, near Ajnala, in a small island, many a Sepoy who had simply fled away from a regiment which was working under the reasonable fear of being disarmed and shot by the Government for suspicion, was hiding himself. Cooper with a loyal body of troops took them prisoner. The entire number, amounting to two hundred and eighty-two, were then conveyed by Cooper to Ajnala. Then came the question what was to be done with them. There was no means of transporting them to a place where they could be tried formally. On the other hand, if they were summarily executed, other regiments and intending rebels might take warning by their fate, and thus, further bloodshed might be prevented. For these reasons, Cooper, fully conscious as he was of the enormous responsibility which he was undertaking, resolved to put

The impression which a visit to these memorials leaves on the mind of an English visitor can be better realised by the following extract from an account published in *The Outlook* (the English journal) on the 3rd of April, 1915, over the signature of one F. G. A. Speaking of the mutiny memories and monuments of Lucknow and Cawnpore, the writer remarks:

"Their mutiny memories are quite distinct, as are the impressions they leave on the pilgrim to these shrines of heroism and devilry. The battered ruins of Lucknow, testifying to a heroism so splendid as to rob even death of its sting, bring an inspiration that is almost joyous. Every crumbling gateway and every gloomy cellar has its tale of heroic endur-

them all to death. Next morning, accordingly, he brought them out in tens and made some Sikhs shoot them. In this way, two hundred and sixteen perished. But, there still remained sixty-six others who had been confined in one of the bastions of the Tahsil. Expecting resistance, Cooper ordered the door to be opened. But not a sound issued from the room; forty-five of them were dead bodies lying on the floor. For, unknown to Cooper, the windows had been closely shut and the wretched prisoners had found in the bastion a second Black-Hole. The remaining twenty-one were shot, like their comrades. 1—8—'57. For this splendid assumption of authority, Cooper was assailed by the hysterical cries of ignorant humanitarians. But Robert Montgomery unanswerably vindicated his character by proving that he had saved the Lahore division."—Holmes's History of the Indian Mutiny, p. 363.

"It is related that, in the absence of tangible enemies, some of our soldiery, who turned out on this occasion, butchered a number of unoffending camp-followers, servants, and others who were huddling together in vague alarm, near the Christian church-yard. No loyalty, no fidelity, no patient good service on the part of these good people could extinguish, for a moment, the fierce hatred which possessed our white soldiers against all who wore the dusky livery of the East."—Kaye and Malleson's Indian Mutiny, vol. II, p. 438.

ance and magnificent defence, and the final relief of the beleaguered garrison wrote such a finis to the story as erased much of its earlier bitterness. . . .

" None of this forgiveness is conceivable in those who visit Cawnpore. Even the sculptured angel over the unspeakable Well bears, on one profile at any rate, an expression of stern condemnation that holds out no promise of pardon. The atmosphere of historic Cawnpore is one of haunting horror and a sadness that will not pass with the years. Time seems powerless to heal this rancour. I care not whether the pilgrim wanders through the beautiful Memorial Gardens (in which, significantly, no native is allowed to enter), feasting his eyes on the *blaze Bougainvillæa,* or resting them in the shade of the peepul and the banyan, or whether he lingers in the strangely Italian-looking Memorial Church and reads the roll of honour that fills a series of mural tablets; everywhere his soul will be filled with gloom and will cry for eternal vengeance on the authors of the massacre and on those who threw the dying with the dead into the awful blackness of the pit. These memories hold nothing but hate and horror, without one redeeming chapter to leaven them with comfort or forgiveness." [7]

The English are mistaken if they think that a reading of the history of the mutiny and the excesses and cruelties indulged in by the British does not excite similar feeling in the minds of the Indians.

[7] It should be noted that this visit took place during the present war and the observations recorded above were penned after the "unique" outburst of loyalty on the part of the Indians in connection with the Great War.

The British can express their feelings freely. The Indians cannot; their feelings must be repressed.

It would, however, be better for both parties to try to wipe off the past in a spirit of mutual trust and mutual good will, which is only possible if England were to cease to pursue a policy of exploiting India and to establish her connection with India on a basis of equality, honesty and justice. That can only be done by treating her as a partner in the Empire and not as a mere "dependency" or "possession."

CHAPTER III

INDIA FROM 1857 TO 1905

PART I — FROM 1857 TO 1885

THE mutiny was quelled. The ringleaders among the mutineers were killed, hanged or shot, and with them a lot of those who were innocent. Many of the rank and file were pardoned, as no government could shoot or hang all those who had taken part in the mutiny. Their number was legion. The British Empire in India was saved, but the East India Company was gone. The system of open pillage was ended. The crown assumed the direct government of India. The Queen's Proclamation and the policy of "mercy and reconciliation" inaugurated by Canning calmed the country.

The Bengalee Babu. The only parts of the country which had received some education on modern lines were the provinces of Bengal, Bombay and Madras. The number of educated men even in these provinces was small. In the work of settlement that followed the mutiny, these educated men found ample scope for their ambition. Men who knew English had the advantage over those who did not. Men with a knowledge of English were few. The posts requiring a knowledge of that language were many. Consequently, the English-knowing Indians were in great demand and secured ample salaries to make them "happy and loyal." The English-knowing Bengalees spread over the whole of Northern India, lately the scene of mutiny, and materially helped in bringing about settled conditions of life. They were the pioneers in every department of governmental activity and were looked to, both by the rulers and the people, for advice and guidance. The Bengalee is a sentimental being. His position under the Government filled him with pride and his gratitude and loyalty were overflowing. The British also liked him because he was useful, intelligent, keen, shrewd, ready to serve, and willing to be of use. He relieved the British officer of much of his intellectual work, and left him ample time for play and rest. Many a departmental head ruled the country with the brain of the "Bengalee Babu." The Bengalee Babu worshipped the Feringhee [1] as *Mai Bap*,[2] and began to imitate him in his tastes. He began to live as the Britisher lived; English life, English manners and customs, became his ideal. Gradually he became very fond of English literature and began to think as an Englishman thought. The Bengalees were the first to send their sons to England for their education and to compete for the I. C. S. (Indian Civil Service) and the I. M. S. (Indian Medical Service). They with the Parsees were the first to qualify for the English bar. In England they lived in an atmosphere of freedom.

[1] A native term equivalent for Europeans.

[2] This is a native expression signifying the highest respect of the speaker towards one whom he considers his superior. Literally it means mother and father.

RAM MOHAN ROY

With freedom in drinking and eating they also learned freedom of thought and expression.

The first generation of the Bengalees was thus Anglicised through and through. They looked down upon their own religion; they thought poorly of Indian society. They knew nothing of their own past history, and they glorified in being "Sahibs."[3] Some of them became Christians. Alarmed at this transformation, Ram Mohan Roy and a few others resolved to stem the tide. For a time they succeeded, but only partially. Be it said to the credit of the Bengalees that a fairly good number refused to be carried down-stream, and in spite of their English education stuck to their own religion and their own customs. They saw a good deal in their society which needed reform; but they declined to make sweeping changes and would not imitate. These veterans laid the foundations of the modern Bengalee literature. They wanted to pour their knowledge, derived from a study of English language and literature, into their own mother tongue, and in order to enlarge the vocabulary of the latter for their work, they had to study Sanskrit. Thus in spite of the Anglification of the first generation of Bengalees, there grew up a class of men imbued with nationalistic tendencies. Ram Mohan Roy, the founder of Brahmo Samaj, was the first nation-builder of Modern India.

For a time the field that was opened for the employment of English-educated Bengalees in Upper India (in the then N. W. Provinces, in the Pun-

[3] *I. e.*, like the English.

jab, in Behar, in Central India, in Rajputana, even in Sindh) checked the growth of these tendencies. The feeling of gratitude and contentment was supreme. The Bengalee was indispensable in almost every department. The reins of practical management were mostly in Bengalee hands, whether it was a court of justice, or a Revenue Commissioner's office, or a commissariat depot, or an adjutant's camp, or the department of land survey, or education. The heads of departments were always English, but the heads of ministerial establishments were generally Bengalees. The English could not do without them. The former did not know the language of the country, nor did they know the character of the people. The Bengalees were thus an absolute necessity. With the spread of a knowledge of the English language, the first generation of English-knowing Indians in every province came to occupy an important position. While the old-fashioned Pandit or Moulvie sulked, the English-knowing Hindu or Mohammedan basked in sunshine and flourished. The British laid down policies and gave orders; the English-knowing Indian saw that they were carried out. They thus came to enjoy the confidence of their masters and imitated their vices.

But what was most important was that they began to think like their English masters. The English read their newspapers; so the Indians started their newspapers. The English met in clubs and churches. So the Indians started Samajes and Sabhas and debating clubs. For a time the English-knowing Indian prided himself in imitating his master. He took his dress, he took his cheroot and pipe, and also his cup and beefsteak. He began to live in houses built and furnished in the English way. He detested Indian life and took pride in being Anglicised. Everything Indian was odious in his eyes. The Indians were barbarians; their religion was a bundle of superstitions; they were dirty people; their customs and manners were uncivilised; they were a set of narrow-minded bigots who did not know that man was born free. So the English set the fashion for them in everything. If their English masters went to church and read the Bible, they did the same. If the English masters indulged in free-thinking, they did the same. They wanted to be like their English masters in every way. Their ambition, however, soon met a check. They could equal the British in drinking and in free-thinking, but they could not aspire to his position and place in the government of the country. Some of them decided to try this in the case of their sons. They sent them to England. A few passed the Indian Civil Service and the Indian Medical Service examinations, others became barristers. Both found out by bitter experience that, however able and clever they might be, whatever their intellectual acquirements, no matter if they were Christians, or semi-Christians, or free-thinkers, there was a limit to their aspirations both in service and out of it. That was the first eye-opener.

In the meantime, the thoughtful among the Indians, who had not taken to English manners, were anxiously watching the flow of the current. They saw the disintegrating and denationalising forces that were at work; they saw that their national edifice was crumbling down brick by brick; everything which they had valued and held sacred was being devastated and treated with contempt and reduced to ashes. Their own children were deserting the old banners to which innumerable generations before them had clung with love and reverence. They saw all this; they were sorry; they wept tears of blood; but they could do nothing. They were powerless before the tide. They tried palliatives, but failed. What was fatal to their pious wishes was that they could not themselves resist the fruits which English education brought in the shape of emoluments and rank and position. They wanted these fruits without the thorns. They soon found that that was impossible, and so they gave up the struggle in despair and became reconciled to the inevitable. What they failed to achieve was, however, brought about by a combination of circumstances which we will briefly enumerate below.

Forces Resisting Denationalisation. 1. The English education imparted in schools and colleges established by the British, and the Christian missions (in some instances supplemented by Indian agencies), opened the gates of Western thought and Western literature to the mass of educated Indians.

2. Some of the British teachers and professors who taught in the schools and colleges consciously and unconsciously inspired their pupils with ideas of freedom as well as nationalism.

SWAMI VIVEKANANDA

3. The over-zeal of the missionaries in their attacks upon Indian religions and Indian thought suggested to Indian minds a closer and deeper study of their own religion and thought.

4. In this they were materially helped by the awakening of Europeans to the thought of the East. The labours of the European savants and their appreciation of Eastern thought kindled a fresh fire in the bosom of Hindus and Mohammedans.

5. The writings of Ram Mohan Roy, Debendra Nath Tagore, Rajendra Lal Mitra, in Bengal, those of Ranade, Vishnu Pandit and others in Mahrashtra, of Swami Dayanand and Sir Syed Ahmad Khan in Upper India, of Madam Blavatsky and the other Theosophists in Madras, brought about a new awakening, which afterwards received an even stronger impetus from the writings and speeches of Mrs. Annie Besant and Swami Vivekananda. This was on the religious and social side mainly, but its national character was unmistakable.

Political Disappointments. The current produced by these causes met another current, which was generated by political disappointments. The aspirations of the educated Indian had met a check. The few successes gained by Indians in the Indian Civil Service examinations alarmed the British, and they sought for means of keeping them out. One of the means adopted was to require that the candidates should not be more than 19 to 21 years of age at the time of examination, an age so young as made it impossible for Indians to come over to England and successfully compete. This raised a howl and cry in Bengal, and the rest of the country followed Bengal. Then came other measures like the Vernacular Press Act of Lord Lytton, and the remission of cotton duties,[4] and so on. The generation educated in England had some experience of the methods of political agitation in that country, and they soon began to organise on those lines. Political agitation on modern lines thus became a fact of Indian life, and English-educated Indians began to talk of liberty and self-government.

Thus were laid the foundations of the national awakening, of which so much has been heard of late. The methods of the English Government in India, their educational system, their press, their laws, their courts, their railways, their telegraphs, their post-offices, their steamers, had as much to do with it as the native love of country, of religion and nation, which had received a temporary check by the crushing defeat of the mutineers in 1857, and by the Indian people's too ready acquiescence in the political and social domination of the foreigner which ensued.

This time, however, the movement was brought into existence by those who had received their inspiration from Europe. Within less than twenty years after the great mutiny, the Nationalist Movement of India was born, almost at the same time and place at which Lord Lytton was presiding at the great Imperial Durbar, and announcing that the great Queen of England was assuming the title of Empress of India. The Durbar reduced the chiefs

[4] In the interests of Lancashire goods.

of India from the position of allies to that of feudatories, but it quite unconsciously and against the intentions of its authors raised in theory the status of the Indian subjects of the Queen to that of citizens of the British Empire. Little did the authors of that Durbar realise the inner significance of the move they were making. That Durbar, we may say, marked the beginning of the movement which filled the educated Indian with the idea of obtaining his rightful place in the Empire. He became articulate and began to assert himself. He was no longer satisfied with the minor positions which he held in the Government of India. He claimed his country as his own, and raised the cry of "India for the Indians." His cry gained strength when he found that the India which he looked down upon in the fifties or sixties, the system of thought and life which he considered barbarous, primitive and old fashioned, and the past which he despised, were after all not so bad as he had thought.

The latter was the contribution of the Brahmo Samaj, the Theosophical Society, the Society for the Resuscitation of Sanskrit Literature, the Bengal Sahitya Parishad, the Maharastra Sabha, the Arya Samaj, the Sanatan Sabhas and other societies of a similar nature. The Bengali and the Mahratta writers, who had carried on researches in Indian history and unearthed valuable documents and written in their respective vernaculars, contributed materially to the growth of this feeling. The Theosophical Society began to praise and justify every Hindu institution and to find science in every custom. In fact, for a time, the thoughtful began to fear lest the pendulum was swinging the other way and we were in the midst of a wave of reaction.

Lord Ripon. India was in this state of fermentation, religious, social and political, when Lord Ripon was appointed to the viceroyalty of India. Lord Ripon was an exceedingly kind man and commanded a broad outlook. He was very lucky in having come on the heels of an exceedingly unpopular Viceroy like Lord Lytton. Lord Lytton was a Tory of pronounced imperial tendencies. Under the inspiration of Disraeli, he had by an unworthy trick on the ruling chiefs of India changed their position from that of allies to that of feudatories; he had gagged the vernacular press by his press legislation; he had blundered into a bloody Afghan war and was responsible for several other reactionary measures. Lord Ripon started by undoing most of what Lord Lytton had done. He repealed the Vernacular Press Act, which at once set the seal of popular approval on his administration. The most important of his achievements were, however, constructive. He formulated a policy of local government, and thus laid the foundations of representative institutions in India; he substituted merit for patronage and jobbery in filling public services, by organising competitive examinations for filling a certain number of posts in the higher branches of the subordinate services; last but not least, he resolved to so alter the criminal law as to place the European and the Indian on an equal footing in the matter of trials.

All this aroused the bitterest anger of the Anglo-

Indian officialdom. The Anglo-Indians opposed every one of these measures. They ridiculed the idea of introducing any measure of local self-government in India, and predicted that that must be the beginning of the end. They called the measure rash and ill-advised and impracticable. The natives were incapable of self-government, they said. Their religious and social differences made it impossible. Officialdom was equally opposed to the filling of any posts in government service by open competition. This would bring in the " Babu," and the " Babu " they had now begun to hate and look down upon. The " Babu " was a " low-caste hybrid," who wrote bad English and talked of liberty and equality, who lacked in qualities of docility and submissiveness, which had so far characterised persons appointed by selection. This interfered materially with the prestige of the Lord of the District, as people could now get " high " appointments under the Government independently of him. Why should the people respect him any more? His was a government by prestige, and measures like these of Lord Ripon would destroy it. So prophesied the heaven-born " white Brahmins." But the worst offence of Lord Ripon was the " Ilbert Bill,"[5] which aimed at placing the European and the Indian on an equal footing in the eyes of the law, and would remove the disabilities of the Indian Magistrate in the matter of the trial of the white men. " Shall we be judged by the Nigger? " " shall he send us to jail? " " shall

[5] Mr. Ilbert was the Law member of the Council of the Governor General and the bill came to be named after him.

he be put in authority over us? Never! It is impossible! Better that British rule in India should end than that we be obliged to submit to such humiliating laws." The whole tribe of the Anglo-Indians (official and non-official) opposed the measure most vehemently, and attacked Lord Ripon as never viceroy was attacked before by his own countrymen in India. They called him insulting names, passed resolutions condemning his administration wholesale, proposed his recall before the expiration of his period of office, and did everything possible to make him feel that they hated him.

His unpopularity among the Anglo-Indians made him popular among the Indians. The press and the platform sang his praise. The country was ablaze with excitement. Never before under British rule had the country been so enthusiastic in political matters. In Lord Ripon, they thought, they had found a political Messiah. They gave him addresses, unharnessed the horses from his carriage, in many places, and otherwise showed their love and regard for him, which exasperated the European community beyond measure. The Europeans saw in all this a menace to their power, and the beginning of the end of imperial despotism in India. They thought they were on the verge of losing India. In Lord Ripon the Indians recognised the first British viceroy who was prepared to make an honest attempt at giving effect to the pledges given and the promises made by Queen Victoria in her famous proclamation of 1858, when the administration of India passed into the hands of the regular British Government. Lord

Ripon lost the battle on the particular measure which had aroused the anger of the European community more than anything else, viz., his proposed amendment of the Criminal Procedure Code. A compromise was made by which the principle of the bill was really abandoned. But he had raised hopes and aspiration which were, so to say, the beginning of political life in India. On the expiration of his term of office, the Indians agitated for an extension of his term, which was not granted. However, they gave him a farewell which still rings in the ears of the older generation of Indians who took part in it, in Calcutta, in Bombay, in Benares, and other places.

Lord Ripon left a permanent impression on the minds of the Indians. Lord Hardinge has won a great deal of popularity, but it is doubtful if he is so universally loved and honoured as Lord Ripon was.

Lord Dufferin. However, the point of the story is, that when Lord Ripon left India, the country was in a state of perturbation. There was a great deal of tension still lingering between the Indian and the European communities. The fire was still smouldering when Lord Dufferin took charge of the office of viceroyalty. He had been brought up in diplomacy. To him diplomacy was like mother's milk. He was a diplomat by birth as well as by training. His mission was to appease the anger of the governing class and in a quiet way to undo what Lord Ripon had done. But he thought that perhaps it might be dangerous to go at it straight. The cry of political liberty and political equality had been raised. It was impossible to satisfy it; yet it might be dangerous to strangle it by force. It was impossible to revive the Vernacular Press Act of Lord Lytton. It was impossible to stifle political life which had sprung up in the atmosphere created by Lord Ripon's policy, and which was making a rather precocious growth. The more it was opposed, ridiculed and despised, the more it thrived. So he decided to guide it and to make it as innocuous as it could be without rousing the suspicions of those who were to be the tools.

PART II. THE BIRTH OF THE INDIAN NATIONAL CONGRESS

Indian National Congress an English Product. It is an undisputed historical fact, that the idea of the Indian National Congress was a product of Lord Dufferin's brain; that he suggested it to Mr. Hume,[6] and that the latter undertook to work it out. We have no means of knowing whether Mr. Hume communicated the fact to all the Indian leaders who joined hands with him in organising it, but in all probability he told some of them. It leaked out, however, in Lord Dufferin's lifetime, was published in the press, brought to his notice and never denied by him. Nor did Mr. Hume, who died only in 1912, ever deny it. It has since been admitted to be true by his biographer, another veteran Congress leader, Sir William Wedderburn.[7] Sir William

[6] Mr. Hume was an ex-secretary of the Government of India who had retired from service.

[7] Sir William Wedderburn is also a retired member of the Government of Bombay, India.

says on page 59 of his life of Mr. Hume: "*Indeed in initiating the National Movement, Mr. Hume took counsel with the viceroy, Lord Dufferin; and whereas he was himself disposed to begin his reform propaganda on the social side, it was apparently by Lord Dufferin's advice that he took up the work of political organisation as the first matter to be dealt with.*" We have no hesitation in accepting the accuracy of the statement made by Sir William Wedderburn as to what Lord Dufferin told Mr. Hume, because we have no doubt of Mr. Hume's sincerity of purpose. Lord Dufferin did evidently tell Mr. Hume that "as head of the Government, he had found the greatest difficulty in ascertaining the real wishes of the people; and that for purposes of administration it would be a public benefit, if there existed some responsible organisation through which the Government might be kept informed regarding the best Indian public opinion." Sir William Wedderburn assures us that "these kindly counsels (*i. e.*, those given by Lord Dufferin) were received with grateful appreciation by all concerned," and "indeed so cordial were the relations" between the officials and the Congress leaders that "Lord Dufferin was approached with a view to the first Congress being held under the presidency of Lord Reay, then Governor of Bombay." We are told that Lord Dufferin welcomed the proposal as showing the desire of the Congress to work in complete harmony with the Government, but he saw many difficulties in accepting the proposal, and so the idea was abandoned. "None the less the first Congress was opened with the friendly sympathy of the highest authorities."

So this is the genesis of the Congress, and this alone is sufficient to condemn it in the eyes of the advanced Nationalists. There is no parallel to this in the history of the world. Who has ever heard of a movement for political liberty being initiated by a despotic government, which is foreign in its agency and foreign in its methods?

Hume, a Lover of Liberty. It is obvious that when Lord Dufferin expected a political organisation to represent the best Indian opinion, it was far from his mind to suggest an organisation that would demand parliamentary government for India, or self-government even on colonial lines. What he evidently aimed at was a sort of an innocuous association which should serve more as a " safety valve " than as a genuine Nationalist organisation for national purposes. Mr. Hume may have meant more. He was a lover of liberty and wanted political liberty for India under the *ægis* of the British crown. He was an English patriot and as such he wanted the continuance of British connection with India. He saw danger to British rule in discontent going underground, and one of his objects in establishing the Congress was to save British rule in India from an impending calamity of the gravest kind which he thought was threatening it at that time. In his reply to Sir Auckland Colvin,[8] he admitted that " a

[8] Sir Auckland Colvin was the Lieutenant Governor of the then North Western Provinces (now the United Province of Agra and Oudh).

safety valve for the escape of great and growing forces generated by" British "connection, was urgently needed, and no more efficacious safety valve than" the "Congress movement could possibly be devised." This correspondence between Sir Auckland Colvin, then Lieutenant Governor of the United Provinces, and Mr. Hume, reveals the whole genesis of the Congress movement, and is so clear and illuminating that no student of Indian politics can afford to neglect it.

It leaves no doubt whatsoever that the immediate motive which underlay the idea of starting the Congress was to save the Empire from "the danger" that loomed ahead "tremendous in the immediate future," "the misery of the masses acted on by the bitter resentment of individuals among the educated class." In the words of Mr. Hume, "no choice was left to those who gave the primary impetus to the movement. The ferment, the creation of Western ideas, education, invention, and appliances, was at work with a rapidly increasing intensity, and it became of paramount importance to find for its products an overt and constitutional channel for discharge, instead of leaving them to fester as they had already commenced to do, under the surface." Mr. Hume further adds that though "in certain provinces and from certain points of view the movement was premature, *yet from the most important point of view, the future maintenance of the integrity of the British Empire,* the real question when the Congress started, was, not is it premature, but is it too late? will the country now accept it?" Indeed, by that test, the events have proved that the Indian National Congress has been a great success, and that either Mr. Hume's reading of the political situation was exaggerated, or that his remedy has been amply justified.

Congress to Save British Empire from Danger. But one thing is clear, that the Congress was started more with the object of saving the British Empire from danger than with that of winning political liberty for India. The interests of the British Empire were primary and those of India only secondary, and no one can say that the Congress has not been true to that ideal. It might be said with justice and reason that the founders of the Indian National Congress considered the maintenance of British rule in India of vital importance to India herself, and therefore were anxious to do everything in their power, not only to save that rule from any danger that threatened it, but even to strengthen it; that with them the redress of political grievances and the political advance of India was only a by-product and of secondary importance. If so, the Congress has been true to its ideal, and no one can find fault with it.

On the strength of an illuminating memorandum found among his papers, Hume's biographer has stated the nature of the evidence that "convinced" Mr. Hume at the time (*i. e.*, about 15 months before Lord Lytton left India) that the British were "in immediate danger of a terrible outbreak." We will give it in Mr. Hume's own words.

"I was shown seven large volumes (corresponding to a certain mode of dividing the country, excluding Burmah, Assam, and some minor tracts) containing a vast number of entries; English abstracts or translations — longer or shorter — of vernacular reports or communications of one kind or another, all arranged according to districts (not identical with ours), sub-districts, sub-divisions, and the cities, towns and villages included in these. The number of these entries was enormous; there were said, at the time, to be communications from over thirty thousand different reporters. I did not count them, they seemed countless; but in regard to the towns and villages of one district of the Northwest Provinces with which I possess a peculiarly intimate acquaintance — a troublesome part of the country, no doubt — there were nearly three hundred entries, a good number of which I could partially verify, as to the names of the people, etc." He mentions that he had the volumes in his possession only for about a week; into six of them he only dipped; but he closely examined one covering the greater portion of the Northwest Provinces, Oudh, Behar, parts of Bundelkund and parts of the Punjab; and so far as possible verified the entries referring to those districts with which he had special personal acquaintance. Many of the entries reported conversations between men of the lowest classes,[9] "all going to show that these poor men were pervaded with a sense of the hopelessness of the existing state of affairs; that they were convinced that they would starve and

[9] The quotations from Hume are taken out of W. Wedderburn's Allan Octavian Hume, the parts enclosed in parenthesis are Wedderburn's.

die, and that they wanted to do *something,* and stand by each other, *and that something meant violence,*" (for innumerable entries referred to the secretion of old swords, spears and matchlocks, which would be ready when required. It was not supposed that the immediate result, in its initial stages, would be a revolt against the Government, or a revolt at all in the proper sense of the word. What was predicted was a sudden violent outbreak of sporadic crimes, murders of obnoxious persons, robbery of bankers, looting of bazaars). "In the existing state of the lowest half-starving classes, it was considered that the first few crimes would be the signal for hundreds of similar ones, and for a general development of lawlessness, paralysing the authorities and the respectable classes. It was considered also, that everywhere the small bands would begin to coalesce into large ones, like drops of water on a leaf; that all the bad characters in the country would join, and that very soon after the bands obtained formidable proportions, a certain small number of the educated classes, at the time desperately, perhaps, unreasonably, bitter against the Government, would join the movement, assume here and there the lead, give the outbreak cohesion, and direct it as a national revolt."

To this, Sir William Wedderburn adds further from his own personal knowledge:

"The forecast of trouble throughout India was in exact accordance with what actually occurred, under my own observation, in the Bombay Presidency, in connection with the Agrarian rising known as the Deccan riots. These began with sporadic gang robberies and attacks on the money lenders, until the bands of dacoits, combining together, became too strong for the police; and the whole military force at Poona, horse, foot, and artillery, had to take the field against them. Roaming through the jungle tracts of the Western Ghauts, these bands dispersed in the presence of military forces, only to reunite immediately at some convenient point; and from the hill stations of Mahableshwar and Matheran we could at night see the light of their campfires in all directions. A leader from the more instructed class was found, calling himself Sivaji, the Second, who addressed challenges to the Government, offered a reward of 500 rupees for the head of H. E. Sir Richard Temple (then Governor of Bombay), and claimed to lead a national revolt upon the lines on which the Mahratta power had originally been founded."

So in the words of these two leaders, the immediate motive of the Congress was to save the British Empire from this danger. There is, however, one difficulty in believing outright that this was the immediate reason of the birth of the Congress. Mr. Hume is said to have seen this evidence at the time he was in the service of the Government, viz., fifteen months before Lord Lytton left India. Between then and the first meeting of the Congress in 1885 intervened a period of about seven years. During this time Lord Ripon was viceroy for five years. The idea of starting a political organisation on the lines of the Congress is said to have originated with Lord Dufferin.

This is a little inconsistent with the theory that the Congress was founded out of fear of a political outbreak and only in the nature of a safety valve. Nor is the latter theory consistent with Mr. Hume's first political manifesto addressed to the graduates of the Calcutta University in March, 1883. This document is so manly in its outspokenness, so true in its principles, that we will quote the whole of it (or at least as much of it as is given in Mr. Hume's biography). Addressing the graduates of the university, Mr. Hume said:

"Constituting, as you do, a large body of the most highly educated Indians, you should, in the natural order of things, constitute also the most important source of all mental, moral, social, and political progress in India. *Whether in the individual or the nation, all vital progress must spring from within, and it is to you, her most cultured and enlightened minds, her most favoured sons, that your country must look for the initiative.* In vain may aliens, like myself, love India and her children, as well as the most loving of these; in vain may they, for her and their good, give time and trouble, money and thought; in vain may they struggle and sacrifice; they may assist with advice and suggestions; they may place their experience, abilities and knowledge at the disposal of the workers, but they lack the essential of nationality, and the real work must ever be done by the people of the country themselves." "Scattered individuals, however capable and however well meaning, are powerless singly. What is needed is union, organisation and a well defined line of action; and to secure these an association is required, armed and organised with unusual care, having for its object to promote the mental, moral, social and political regeneration of the people of India. Our little army must be *sui generis* in discipline and equipment, and the question simply is, how many of you will prove to possess, in addition to your high scholastic attainments, the unselfishness, moral courage, self-control, and active spirit of benevolence which are essential in all who should enlist?"

Even truer and nobler are the sentiments in the final appeal which ended this letter and which runs thus:

"As I said before, you are the salt of the land. *And if amongst even you, the élite, fifty men can not be found with sufficient power of self-sacrifice, sufficient love for and pride in their country, sufficient genuine and unselfish heartfelt patriotism to take the initiative, and if needs be, devote the rest of their lives to the cause, then there is no hope for India.* Her sons must and will remain mere humble and helpless instruments in the hands of foreign rulers, for '*they who would be free, themselves must strike the blow.*' And if even the leaders of thought are all either such poor creatures, or so selfishly wedded to personal concerns, that they dare not or will not strike a blow for their country's sake, then justly and rightly are they kept down and trampled on, for they deserve nothing better. *Every nation secures precisely as good a government as it merits.* If you, the picked men, the most highly educated of the nation, can not, scorning personal ease and selfish ends, *make a resolute struggle to secure freedom for yourselves and your country,* a more impartial administration, a larger share in the management of your own affairs, then we, your friends, are wrong, and our adversaries right; then are Lord Ripon's aspirations for your good, fruitless and visionary; then, at present, at any rate, all hopes of progress are at an end, and India truly neither lacks nor deserves any better government than she now enjoys. Only, if this be so, let us hear no more factious, peevish complaints that you are kept in leading strings, and treated like children, for you will have proved yourselves such. *Men know how to act.* Let there be no more complaints of Englishmen being preferred to you in all important offices, for if you lack that public spirit, that highest form of altruistic devotion that leads men to subordinate private ease to the public weal, that true patriotism that has made Englishmen what they are, then rightly are these preferred to you, and rightly and inevitably have they become your rulers. And rulers and taskmasters they must continue, let the yoke gall your shoulders ever so sorely, until you realise and stand prepared to act upon the eternal truth, *whether in the case of individuals or nations, self-sacrifice and unselfishness are the only unfailing guides to freedom and happiness.*"

The capitals and italics are, except in two cases, ours. In the original there are only two italics, (1) the word *themselves* in the sentence "they who would be free, *themselves* must strike the blow," and, (2) "*Men* know how to act." Now these are not the words of a diplomat, much less those of a hypocrite. Mr. Hume was too noble not to mean what he said, and the present writer has no doubt but that Mr. Hume was absolutely sincere in what he said. He had a passion for liberty. His heart bled at the sight of so much misery and poverty as prevailed in India, and which according to him was preventable by good government. He burned with indignation at the "cowardly" behaviour of his countrymen towards Indians, and he could not help feeling ashamed at the way in which pledges given and promises made were being ignored. He was an ardent student of history and knew full well that no government, whether national or foreign, had conceded to popular demands without pressure from below. In the case of an alien government, the chances were even still more meagre. He therefore wanted the Indians "to strike" for their liberty if they wanted it. The first step was to organise. So he advised organisation.

Nor are we prepared to believe that men like Ranade, Tilak, Naoroji, W. C. Bonnerjea, Ajudhia Nath, and Tyabji, were only tools in the hands of the Britishers. No, we do not think so. They were all true and good patriots. They loved their country and they started the Congress with the best of motives. It is possible that with some British sympathisers, the interests of the British Empire were primary, and they sided with the Congress because they believed that thereby they could best secure the Empire; but the writer of this book knows from personal experience how deeply the love of humanity and liberty is embedded in the hearts of some Britishers, and he is compelled to believe that at least some of those who showed their sympathy with the Congress were of that kind.

The Imperialist Junker and Jingo calls such men "Little Englanders," but the truth is that their hearts are too big to be imperial. They believe in humanity, and in liberty being the birthright of every human being. In their eyes a tyrant, one who robs others of their liberty, one who bases his greatness on the exploitation of others, or deprives them of their rights by might or clever diplomacy, does not cease to be so by the fact of his being their countryman. They are patriots themselves and will shed the last drop of their blood in the defence of their liberty, and in the defence of their country's liberty and independence, but their patriotism does not extend to the point of *applauding* their country's robbing others of theirs. Yes, there are Britons who are sincere friends of the cause of liberty all over the globe. They deplore that their country should be ruling India at all, and if it were in their power, they would at once withdraw from India. Some of these sympathise with the Indian Nationalists in all sincerity, and have done so ever since the Indian National Congress was started, or even from before that time. It is no fault of theirs, if the Indian Nationalist Movement has not been such a success as they would have wished it to be, and if it has not been able to achieve anything very tangible. The fault is purely that of the Indians, and of the Indians alone, or of the circumstances.

Mr. Hume was quite sincere in his motives, but he forgot that a political organisation started at the instance or even with the approval of the rulers whose power and emoluments it proposed to curtail, whose despotism and principles it questioned, in short, whom it proposed to displace and dethrone, was an anomaly; it was unnatural. In their desire to have an easy and unopposed start, the Indian founders of the National Congress forgot their history, and consequently ignored the truth that "those who wanted to be free must themselves strike the blow," and that it was monstrous to expect those against whom the blow was aimed to bless the striker and the striking. We do not agree with Mr. Gokhale that "no Indian could have started the Indian National Congress" and that "if the founder of the Congress had not been a great Englishman and a distinguished ex-official, such was the official distrust of political agitation in those days that the authorities would have at once found some way or other to suppress the movement."

First, political agitation did not start with the Congress. It had been started before and no attempt to suppress it had succeeded. Second, the distrust of political agitation in India was not greater in those days than it is now and has been during the life of the Congress. But if it be true that the movement could not have been started by an Indian or by the combined efforts of many Indians, all we can say is that that itself would be proof of its having been started before time and on wrong foundations.

Had not Mr. Hume said that "whether in the individual or the nation, all vital progress must spring from within," and that it was "to her own sons that the country must look for the initiative?" Did not Mr. Hume say in his manifesto of 1883 that "in vain may aliens like myself love India . . . in vain may they struggle and sacrifice . . . they may assist with advice and suggestion, but they lack the *essential* of nationality, and the real work must ever be done by the people of the country themselves?"

These may be only truisms, but they are fundamental and any political effort made in defiance of them must be futile and impotent. The Indian leaders of the Congress have never fully realised the absolute truth of these principles and the result is the comparatively poor record of the Congress. In his original manifesto issued in 1883, Mr. Hume wanted fifty Indians "with sufficient power of self-sacrifice, sufficient love for and pride in their country, sufficient genuine and unselfish heartfelt patriotism to take the initiative and if needs be to devote the rest of their lives to the cause."

Of course there were many times fifty men of that kind in the country, even then, who were devoting their lives to the service of their country, but not in the political line. It took the Congress and the country, by working on Congress lines, more than twenty years to produce fifty, many times fifty, such men to devote their lives to the political cause.

But unfortunately these are neither in the Congress, nor of the Congress. Barring Mr. Dadabhai Naoroji and the late Mr. Gokhale, who among the living Congress leaders can be said to have devoted their lives, in the way Mr. Hume wanted them to do, to the Congress cause? Within the last thirty years India has produced many noble sons who have given their all in the service of the Motherland. They come from all provinces, all religions, all denominations, and all castes. But very few of them have ever been active in the Congress or for the Congress. Within the same period many Indians have given away many hundreds of thousands of rupees, some the whole earnings of a lifetime, in aid of education or for other public or charitable purposes; but the Congress work has always languished for want of funds. The British Committee of the Indian National Congress, located in London, have never had sufficient money to do their work decently. The expenses of the British Committee have largely fallen on Sir William Wedderburn. He and Mr. Hume between them spent quite a fortune on the movement. No single Indian is said to have spent even a fraction of that. The question naturally arises,—why has it been so? The answer is obvious. The movement did not appeal to the nation. The leaders lacked that faith which alone makes it possible to make great sacrifices for it.

In the early years of the Congress there was a great deal of enthusiasm for it among the English educated Indians. So long as no attempts were made to reach the masses and carry on the propaganda among the people, the officials expressed their sympathy with the movement. Lord Dufferin even invited the members as "distinguished visitors" to a garden party at Government House, Calcutta, when the Congress held its second session in that city in 1886. In 1887 the Governor of Madras paid a similar compliment to them at Madras,[10] but in 1888 when Mr. Hume adopted the methods and tactics of the Corn-Law Leaguers of England, down came the hand of the Government; and then the Congress movement at once adopted an apologetic tone and abandoned the only method by which it could make itself heard with effect. Why? Because, in the words of Mr. Hume, there were no "*men* who could act."

The Congress Lacked Essentials of a National Movement. Ever since then the Congress has cared more for the opinion of the Government and the officials than for truth or for the interests of the country. Again the question arises, why? And the reply is, because the leaders had neither sufficient political consciousness nor faith. They had certain political opinions, but not beliefs for which they were willing to suffer. They were prepared to urge the desirability of certain reforms in the government of the country, even at the risk of a certain amount of official displeasure, but they were not prepared to bear persecutions, or suffer for their cause.

[10] These compliments have been renewed of late. The Congress held at Madras in 1914 was attended by the British Governor of the Presidency.

Either they did not know they had a cause, or they were wanting in that earnestness which makes men suffer for a cause. Or, to be charitable, they thought that the country was not prepared for an intense movement and considered it better to have something than nothing. They perhaps wanted to educate the country in political methods and bring about a political consolidation of all the national forces, before undertaking an intensified movement. But with the greatest possible respect for the founders of the Indian National Congress, or for those who a few years ago took up the control of the movement, we cannot help remarking that by their own conduct they showed that their movement lacked the essentials of a national movement.

A movement does not become national by the mere desire of its founders to make it so. In the opinion of the writer it is a mistake to start *a national political movement* unless those who start it are prepared to make great sacrifices for it. A halting, half-hearted political movement depending on the sympathy and good will of the very class against whom it is directed, consulting their wishes at every step, with its founders or leaders trembling for their safety and keeping their purse strings tight, only doing as much as the authorities would allow and as would not interfere in any way with their own personal interests and comforts and incomes, is from its very nature detrimental to real national interests. A political movement is mischievous in its effects if its leaders do not put a sufficient amount of earnestness into it to evoke great enthusiasm among their followers, such as would prepare them for great sacrifices for the cause on the one hand, and on the other, produce a certain amount of fear of unpleasant consequences in those against whom it is directed. For this it is necessary that the leaders should be prepared to suffer for the cause. The sacrifice of money is the least proof of earnestness which a believer in any cause can give.

It is a fact that the English friends of the movement showed more earnestness than many of the Indian leaders. They spent their own money over it and they incurred the displeasure of their countrymen and the odium of being called traitors to their own country. Mr. Hume was "in deadly earnest." He started the movement with the good will of the authorities and waited for results for two years. When, however, he found that "the platonic expressions of sympathy by the authorities were a mockery," that nothing was done to lessen the "misery of the masses" and to relieve their sufferings and redress their grievances, he decided to put more intensity into the movement. He undertook to instruct the Indian nation and rouse them to a sense of their right and to a sense of the wrong that was being done to them. In his opinion, "the case was one of extreme urgency, for the deaths by famine and pestilence were counted not by tens of thousands or by hundreds of thousands, but by millions."[11] He concluded that "in order to *constrain the Government* to move, the leaders of

[11] Mr. Hume's biography by Sir William Wedderburn, p. 62.

the Indian people must adopt measures of exceptional vigour, following the drastic methods pursued in England by Bright and Cobden in their great campaign on behalf of the people's food." So, like Cobden, Hume decided that since the attempt of the Congress leaders to instruct the Government had failed and since the Government had refused to be instructed by them, the next step was "to instruct the nations, the great English nation in its island home, *and also the far greater nation* of this vast Indian continent, so that every Indian that breathes upon the sacred soil of this our motherland, shall become our comrade and coadjutor, our supporter and if need be *our soldier, in the great war that we, like Cobden and his noble band, will wage for justice, for our liberties and our rights.*" [12]

Hume's Political Movement. Now these were noble words, pointing out the only political weapon that ever succeeds against autocratic governments. We are told by Mr. Hume's biographer that "in pursuance of such a propaganda in India, Mr. Hume set to work with his wonted energy, appealing for funds to all classes of the Indian community, distributing tracts, leaflets and pamphlets, sending out lecturers and calling meetings both in large towns and in country districts. Throughout the country over one thousand meetings were held, at many of which over five thousand persons were present, and arrangements were made for the distribution of half a million pamphlets, translations

[12] Mr. Hume's biography by Sir W. W., p. 63.

into twelve Indian languages being circulated of two remarkable pamphlets, showing by a parable the necessary evils of absentee state landlordism, however benevolent the intention." [13]

That was true political work, done with a real political insight. If it had been persevered in, the history of the Congress would have been different and perhaps the revolutionary party would never have been born or would have been born earlier. In either case the country would have been farther ahead in politics than it is now. What, however, actually happened was that the Government was at once moved to hostility. Lord Dufferin spoke of the Congress in terms of contempt "as the infinitesimal minority," at a Calcutta dinner. Sir Auckland Colvin stirred up the Mohammedans, organised an Anti-Congress Association and denounced the Congress in no measured terms, as mischievous, disloyal, and much before the time.

Congress Overawed. Mr. Hume started to explain in an apologetic tone. It was at this time that he came out with the "safety valve" theory. The propaganda was at once abandoned, never to be resumed in the history of the movement. The movement in England failed for want of funds. The movement in India collapsed for want of perseverance, vigour and earnestness. Here again we are disposed to think that Mr. Hume's subsequent conduct was influenced more by the fears and half-heartedness of the Indian leaders than by his own judgment. If the Indian leaders had stuck to their

[13] Biography, p. 63.

guns and pushed on their propaganda, the country would have supplied funds and would have rallied round them. Perhaps there might have been a few riots and a few prosecutions. But that would have drawn the attention of the British public to Indian conditions more effectively than their twenty-eight years of half-hearted propaganda in England did. The political education of the people would have been more rapid and the movement would have gained such a strength as to make itself irresistible. It is possible, nay, probable, that the Government would have suppressed the movement. But that itself would have been a victory and a decided and effective step in the political education of the people. The revolutionary movement would have come earlier and the Government would have seen the wisdom of conciliating the moderates much earlier than 1909. What was given to us in 1909 might have been given twenty years earlier. The Mohammedans would have been happy to get in 1889 what they got in 1909. The Indian leaders, however, thought that they were not sufficiently strong and that the movement stood the chance of being suppressed. They gave in and abandoned the only effective weapon they had forged to get redress of political grievances.

No nation and no political party can ever be strong enough to make their voice effective, unless and until they put forward a sufficient amount of *earnestness* (not bluff) to convince their opponents that in case their demands are trifled with, the consequences might be serious to both parties. The history of political advance in self-governed countries like England, Germany, France, etc., amply proves this. No political agitation need be started unless those who are engaged in it are prepared to back it by the power of the purse and the power of conviction.

Congress Agitation in England. The Congress overawed in 1888 and 1889, failed in both respects. So far as the first is concerned, why, that has been a theme of lamentation, appeals, and wailings from year to year. Friends in England, whether in or outside the British Committee, have lamented it in pathetic terms. The Congress agitation in England has never been effective. The Congress has had precious little influence on English public opinion, and although the British Committee of the Congress have had an office and an organ in London for the last 25 years or more, their influence in English politics has been almost nil. But for the generosity of Mr. Hume and Sir William Wedderburn, the Congress office in London might have been long ago closed. The leaders of the Congress have talked very much of their implicit faith in the English nation; they have held out hopes of our getting a redress of our wrongs if we could only inform the British people of the condition of things prevalent in India; yet the efforts they have put forward to achieve that end have been puerile and paltry. There is a party of Indian politicians who do not believe in agitation in England, but the leaders of the Congress and those who have controlled the organisation in the last 30 years do not profess to belong to that party.

We shall now try to explain why this has been so.

Causes of Failure of the Congress. (1). The movement was neither inspired by the people nor devised or planned by them. It was a movement not *from within.* No section of the Indian people identified themselves with it so completely as to feel that their existence as honourable men depended on its successful management. The movement was started by an Englishman, at the suggestion of an English pro-consul. The Indians, who professed to lead it, were either actually in government service or in professions allied to government service and created by the Government. A good many of the latter aspired to offices under the Government or to a recognition of their merit and public spirit by the Government. They were patriotic enough to give a part of their time and energy to the movement, so long as it did not clash with their own interests, so long as they were not required to mar their careers for it, or so long as it did not demand heavy sacrifices from them. We do not question either their motives or their patriotism, but it was not sufficiently intense to induce them to stake their *all* on it.

(2). The movement lacked the essentials of a popular movement. The leaders were not in touch with the people. Perhaps they did not even want to come in touch with them. Their propaganda was confined to a few English-educated persons, was carried on in English and was meant for the ears of the authorities rather than for the people. The leaders always felt shy of the masses, made no efforts to reach them, and systematically discouraged the younger men from doing the same. Some of them have openly opposed efforts in this direction.

(3). The leaders failed to inspire enthusiasm among the people, either by their own failure to make sacrifices, or by the triviality of their sacrifices. Their ordinary life, their income, their prosperity, and their luxuries were in no way affected by the movement. There were only two exceptions to this, viz., Dadabhai Naoroji and Gokhale. The sacrifices of Messrs. Hume and Wedderburn shamed the people, but failed to appeal to their imagination. In fact, they roused the anger of the people against the leaders and created distrust. The spectacle of leaders accepting high offices they were offered under the Government added to this distrust.

(4). The movement was neither confined to a select few, nor open to all. While the people were expected to add to the spectacular side of the show by their presence in large numbers, by crowded meetings, by cheers and applause, they were never given a hand in the movement. Differences of opinion were always discouraged and free discussion was never allowed. It was neither a public forum, nor a private meeting of the select few. In the latter case it would have been less expensive and would have saved money for work in England. In the former case it would have been more effective.

(5). A national movement, demanding only a few concessions and not speaking of the liberties of the nation and of its ideals, is never an effective movement. It is at best an opportunist movement. It is mischievous in so far as it diverts attention from substantial *nation building* and *character making.* It brings fame without sacrifice. It opens opportunities for treacheries and hypocrisies. It enables some people to trade in the name of patriotism. No political movement can be entirely free from these disadvantages, but the greatest mischief which a political movement lightly handled and led does, is that it delays the development of the people on normal lines by raising hopes which are baseless and can never be realised by means recommended and methods adopted.

PART III. THE BIRTH OF THE NEW NATIONALIST MOVEMENT

The National Movement in India continued on its placid and humdrum course until Lord Curzon's ridicule of the movement convinced the people that the political methods of the Congress were quite powerless to bring them any relief against the despotism that trampled upon all their rights and sensibilities. This led to a deeper and a closer study of the political problem on the part of men who had convictions as distinguished from opinions, who had faith as against opportunism, who wanted a soul for their people, rather than a few more posts under the Government. They discovered that the movement had suffered not only by the adoption of wrong methods and by want of sacrifice on the part of leaders, but by their failure to grasp principles and to formulate ideals. Hence the cry of *Swadeshi* and *Swaraj*.[14]

Swadeshi and Swaraj. No sooner was the cry raised than the country was swept by a wave of political activity which deeply and intimately influenced the proceedings of the Congress in 1905 and 1906. Calcutta might have witnessed in 1906 what Surat did in 1907, but for the sagacity and patriotism of Dadabhai, who rose equal to the occasion and blessed the cry for self-government. He declared in the words of Sir Henry Campbell-Bannerman, the British Premier, that good government could never be a substitute for self-government. So far good government had been the ideal of the Congress. At the Calcutta session of 1906 it was changed to self-government,— and from the mouth of a man who had devoted his whole life to the political cause. That is the date of the birth of the real National Movement in India.

The *Surat Fiasco*[15] was, among other causes, brought about by the fear that the so-called moderate leaders wanted to go back past what had been done in 1906. There is no doubt that they had gone back in spirit, though perhaps not in letter. The enthusiasm, created by popular propaganda of the Congress in 1888, was killed by the reaction that followed in subsequent years. The same thing would have happened in 1907 but for the fact that

[14] Swadeshi means country-made, and Swaraj means self-government or self-rule.

[15] The Congress session held at Surat in December, 1907, ended in a split preceded by a disorderly meeting.

this time the movement was sufficiently intense to claim its martyrs.

The high ideals embodied in Swadeshi and Swaraj were the ideals worked out by the sons of India: the miseries of the motherland had given an impetus to the idea, but the idea itself stood on higher ground. It was not the redress of grievances that filled the mind of the people, but the desire for liberty. It was not concessions they wanted, but liberty. Liberty is not a thing of the earth, and therefore it can neither be given nor accepted as a gift. It has to be won. People felt that, and were prepared to realise that in their lives.

After more than twenty years of more or less futile agitation for concessions and redress of grievances, they had received stones in place of bread. Lord Ripon was succeeded by a Curzon. People saw that a sort of mist, a deep, covering fog, had prevented them from seeing ahead. They had been wandering in pursuit of vain things. The haven had been concealed from their vision and the result was that their tiny bark had been following a wrong course. The waters were stormy and the sea was heavy, but no ship could reach its destination unless the mariners and sailors in charge knew what their goal was, and unless they were prepared to put forth all they had in them to carry the bark through. So far, the bark had been sailing under misleading stars, without a compass to guide the captain. Now the compass was found and with the finding of the compass the aspect changed. Ideas inspire men. Ideals prepare them to breast martyrdom. The ideal of Swaraj found men ready to suffer for it, to meet death like martyrs. The new movement has inspired a class of men whose life is filled with that idea and that idea alone. They are the worshippers of Swaraj; they love their motherland above everything else. They do not want office, or incomes, or recognition, or applause. What they want is liberty, not for themselves, because that they might get perhaps by settling in other countries, but for their beloved country. High Court Judgeships, Civil Service, Councils, mean nothing to them.

The founders of the Indian National Congress began their movement under inspiration of government and under the shadow of the high offices they held or aspired to under that government, but the founders and inspirers of the National Movement started their propaganda by boycotting government and government patronage. The former wanted high offices, the latter despised those who held them. The former asked for concessions, the latter rejected them. The former wanted Councils, the latter would have nothing to do with them. The former appealed to the British Government and the British nation, the latter appealed to their own people and to their own patriotism and to their God. The former were led by the British, the latter by pure Indians. The former would not do anything which would mar their careers, the latter threw away their chances like poisoned bread. The former lived in bungalows, revelled in drawing rooms, velvet-covered chairs, were attended by liveried servants, ate at well-furnished tables, entertained governors and migistrates; the latter gave up even the little comforts they had, changed trousers for *dhotis,* coats for *chapkans* or *kurtas* (shirts), overcoats for blankets, and boots for ordinary Swadeshi shoes. The former owed their prosperity in life, their positions, and their comforts, to the British system, and were therefore under obligation to the British; but the latter chose the path of poverty and destitution to avoid obligations. They threw away their chances deliberately and with the conviction that that was the right thing to do. The former cared for wines, for children, and for home. The latter gave up all, to devote themselves completely to the cause and to the motherland. The former had produced only two full time workers for the cause in the course of 22 years, the latter produced virtually hundreds and thousands in less than two years. The former worked under the best auspices, the latter started their work under overhanging clouds, which soon burst and swept away many of them into prisons.

Is it any wonder that under such inspiration the movement spread like wildfire and assumed wide proportions? Life met life. Forces met forces. Conflict and clash resulted in fatal accidents to either party. The casualties on the side of the Nationalists have been tremendously heavy and out of all proportion to their number, but judging the conflict by the resources, no one need hesitate in saying that the moral victory lies with the Nationalists. Within less than five years of their propaganda, they forced the hand of the Government to make concessions which could not be even thought of in 1905. The Congress leaders claim credit for themselves and so does the Government; but the verdict of impartial and unbiased historians will be otherwise.

Lord Morley would rally the moderates because there were extremists in the land. In the absence of the so-called extremists, the moderates were extremists and the Government and its agents looked down upon them. The Anglo-Indian statesman and his confidant, the moderate Congress leader, say that the extremists are few, that most of them are those good-for-nothings, who could do nothing at the universities, or with their lives; that they are maniacs and men who have lost all sense of right and wrong.

Men who have Inspired the Movement. But look at the men who have inspired the movement, some of whom are leading it even to-day. Is Arabinda Ghosh a failure? Is Har Dayal a failure? Were the nine deportees from Bengal failures? How many high-class graduates have been hanged; how many are in jail! Look at their university records and look at their prospects, and then say if you can call them "malcontents" or men who have arisen against the Government because they could not prosper under it. Their propaganda has compelled the Government to adopt the severest repressive measures open to a foreign government. The penal code has been amended to make the definition of sedition more comprehensive. The criminal procedure code has been amended to facilitate convictions and to accelerate trials. Provisions have been added to enable magistrates to award summary imprisonment for failure to give security for good behaviour asked for on political grounds. A Seditious Meetings Act has been enacted to make open propaganda impossible. An Explosives Act has been placed on the statute book. A Press Law has been passed to muzzle the press. Spies and detectives have been employed out of number. Teachers, professors, friends, pupils, class-fellows, parents, have all been requisitioned to crush the movement. The number of publications confiscated under the Press Act, the convictions for sedition, for seditious murders, for dacoities and for keeping arms, the sentences for failure to find securities for good behaviour, all continue to grow. The cry is, "Still they come!" In prisons the political prisoner has been subjected to horrible treatment; one committed suicide and another lost his senses in the Andamans. Many a tale of misery and wretchedness, of torture and of insults comes from the prisons in India, but still the movement is far from being crushed.

There is evidence that new recruits join the secret propaganda every year and take the place of those hanged or imprisoned. A number has exiled themselves and are carrying on their propaganda in distant lands under very discouraging and depressing circumstances. The man who says that the movement is dead or dying must be a liar or a fool. The movement is alive and possibly as vigorous as it ever was. It has captured the imagination of the younger generation. And at least 75 per cent. of the students in India and in England sympathise with this party. Almost all are Anti-Congress. Even those who are not Nationalists do not like the Congress and feel no obligation towards it, because the Congress failed to communicate high principles and lay down high ideals, and because it failed to create that spirit of self-sacrifice, that willingness to suffer, without which no national movement can grow, prosper, and inspire.

The failures of the Congress evolved the Nationalist Movement. The Congress did its work that way. It brought conviction home that no amount of prayers, resolutions, protests, memorials, could move the autocratic bureaucracy in India, and no amount of petitions were likely to make any impression upon the people in England. The fact that the Congress leaders would not make sacrifices for the Congress cause, though they would give large amounts of money for educational purposes and other charities, forced people to think that they themselves had no faith in the Congress propaganda or in the Congress methods, though they lacked the courage to say so or to change their methods. It was perhaps unreasonable to expect that of the kind of men that led the Congress. Most of them loved their country and were public spirited; they had given proof of it, good and sufficient, in other sides of national activity, in the cause of social reform, in the cause of public education, in industrial propaganda. Outside the Congress they have done enough to create an atmosphere which was bound to bring about the development of the political movement along the lines on which it eventually did develop in 1905.

The Nationalist child was, so to say, brought up on the lap of the old Congress man and fed on the food provided by him; though, strange enough, this bringing up and this feeding produced results for which the Congressman was not prepared and which shocked him a bit. The first shock over, some of them were happy to have lived to see the day, and blessed the movement. Some made up their minds to throttle it, but soon found that it was not in their power to do so. The worst they could do was to condemn it and to denounce it. All they could achieve was to cut the new movement, shake off all responsibility for it, and thus secure their own safety. We do not say that they did it to save their skins. But fortunately for them their convictions led them the way their safety lay. In their heart of hearts they blessed the new movement and were heartily glad that it came. It acted and reacted on their own movement. It made it possible for them to put strength and force into their demands for concessions. Whenever an extremist leader recanted or used compromising language, they were sorry. They wanted the movement to continue and to live, though they would not join it and though they believed that it was harmful to the country in some respects. They deplore the lack of enthusiasm and sacrifice in their own ranks, but they admire the selflessness of the extremists and respect their real leaders. An Arabinda Ghosh and a Tilak simply compel their admiration and respect. Whatever the shortcomings of Har Dayal may be, he is a unique personality.

We have stated wherein the new movement differed from the old, and we have also stated what its dominant note is. We would now like to examine how it intended to proceed and how its hands were forced to do the things it has done since.

Lord Curzon and Indian Education. We have already hinted that Lord Curzon's policy and his utterances helped a great deal in the birth of the new movement. When Lord Curzon came to India, he formulated a rather ambitious programme of reforms to be introduced into the administration of the country. One of these reforms related to education.

Every one in the country, who has had anything to do with education in India, was of opinion that the country was very backward in education and that the system of education there in vogue was defective. It laid too great stress on the literary side and did not fit people for the battle of life; it gave undue importance to the English language and Western modes of thought, at the cost of the vernaculars and the indigenous civilisation of the country; it encouraged "cram" at the cost of real merit; it produced a class of imitators and left little scope or none for originality; it invited third class men from England to fill the highest positions in the educational service of the country, and placed the best native intellect and talent under them to starve and rot for want of opportunities; it did not recognise the duty of the Government to look after the education of the child from the beginning until he was fit to fight his own way in the world.

The educational system of the country required radical changes, but what was most needed was that the Government should be prepared to spend adequate sums of money for its spread and in order to make it efficient. Lord Curzon's pronouncements and programme therefore raised great hopes in the minds of the people. His University Commission was simply flooded with suggestions and statements from Indians and Anglo-Indians. The two classes, however, discussed the matter from entirely different standpoints: The Indians wanted greater facilities for education, more schools, more colleges, more masters, more stipends, an extension of primary school education, abler and better-paid teachers, freedom of private enterprise, ample provision for technical and industrial education; but what they wanted most and cared for most was that education should be more nationalised and humanised. The Anglo-Indians wanted a curtailment of the educational opportunities, a greater and stricter control of private enterprise, a raising of university standards, and a system of education which would curb the rising generation and make them more easily amenable to discipline and obedience.

Lord Curzon did go into all these questions, but the decision arrived at convinced the educated Indians that the motive which underlay Lord Curzon's policy was the tightening of government control, the strangling of all independence in matters educational, and the eventual weakening of all national movement and national sentiment.

Lord Curzon's Secret Educational Conference. The fact that he admitted no Indian to the meeting of the Secret Educational Conference held at Simla, when he formulated the government policy, strengthened that idea. His University Legislation shocked the country beyond measure and left no doubt whatsoever that what he aimed at was a complete official control of all education in India. Educated Indians read between the lines and concluded that it was a mistake to look to the Government to do things or to follow a policy which might quicken the national pulse, strengthen the Nationalist sentiment, or add to the efficiency of the people so as to fit them to stand on their legs and desire to get rid of the leading strings in which they were held by the British.

Indians and Lord Curzon at Cross Purposes. Indians saw that they and Lord Curzon were at cross-purposes. They aimed at self-government and freedom; Lord Curzon aimed at prolongation of the period of their bondage and the permanence of the existing political conditions. We wanted independence; he wanted us to be dependent on the British. We wanted to quicken the pace of national advance; he wanted to slacken it. We wanted to be assertive and self-reliant; he wanted us to be submissive and in permanent control and tutelage. We wanted to go forward, he mistrusted us. We wanted a policy of honest confidence; instead of that he inaugurated a policy of suspicion. We wanted unity, he proceeded to bring into existence fresh causes of friction between community and community. We wanted the marshalling of our forces in the common cause, he proceeded to divide us and to keep us apart. We wanted consolidation, and he started active disintegration. We wanted an extension of representative government, Lord Curzon did his best to discredit the institutions that had been granted and to set back the hands of the clock.

The Congress Deputation to England in 1905. The leaders of the Indian National Congress saw all this; they resisted Lord Curzon's policy rather boldly; they spoke with courage; they sought his patronage and sent their president to wait on him. Lord Curzon refused to see him and thus slapped the Congress in the face. He characterised their activities as the letting off of "gas." Their resolutions he looked upon with contempt because, as he said, nothing had ever come out of them. The leaders felt offended, they fretted and foamed. But all they resolved to do was to appeal to the British public. So a deputation was sent to England in 1905 to place the grievances of India before the British public.

This deputation was composed of Messrs. Gokhale and the writer of this book. They addressed a large number of meetings in Great Britain, made many friends, saw some politicians; but they were not very hopeful as to the results. One of them on his return (the present writer) struck an unmistakable note of despondency. He frankly told his people that the British democracy was too busy with their own affairs to do anything for them, that the

British press was not willing to champion Indian aspirations, that it was hard to get a hearing in England, and that the influence and the credit of the Anglo-Indians was too strong to be met successfully by the necessarily inadequate agitation which the Congress could set up in England. On his return to India the message which he brought to his people was, that if they really cared for their country, they would have to strike the blow for freedom themselves, and that they would have to furnish unmistakable proofs of their earnestness.

His message was in no way different from what Mr. Hume had told the graduates of the Calcutta University in 1883, or in his pamphlets "The Star in the East" and the "Old Man's Hope."

The Congress of 1905. This was the first time that an Indian publicist had spoken in that strain. The *swadeshi* and *boycott* had already been started in Bengal during his absence from India. Even Mr. Gokhale approved of the boycott as a political weapon. So the message which he brought fell on willing and sympathetic ears. The country was in a mood to listen to it, and it did listen. The Congress Session of 1905, held at Benares,[16] gave an opportunity for comparing notes and for settling a programme. The reception accorded to Mr. Gokhale and the rather uproarious meetings of the Subjects Committee afforded ample evidence of the temper of the people. Gokhale was cautious, careful, but enthusiastic. His presidential address was

[16] Presided over by the Honourable Mr. G. K. Gokhale, a member of the Viceroy's Council.

inspiring, though strictly moderate. His Bombay friends, however, would not let him go sufficiently far. The very first night the Subjects Committee sat, it appeared that a split was inevitable and the proceedings could not be as unanimous and harmonious as was customary. The old Congress leaders were accustomed to unanimity, but the younger generation soon convinced them that unanimity on the old lines was impossible.

When the meeting of the Subjects Committee broke up after its deliberation on the first night, no unanimity had been reached with regard to a resolution welcoming the visit of the Prince of Wales (the present King) to India. The dissentionists threatened to oppose it in the Congress. The reception committee and the older leaders were all furious, threatened all sorts of retributions, and predicted all sorts of evil consequences, but the younger men would not listen. The whole of the morning was spent in efforts to induce them to withdraw their opposition, but young Bengal refused to agree. The meeting was delayed; Gokhale then made a personal appeal to the Mahratta and the Punjab leaders, and they prevailed on their Bengalee friends to absent themselves from the meeting and let the resolution be passed in their absence. The resolution relating to Swadeshi,[17] boycott, and national education, again evoked lively discussion resulting in compromise, wherein the principles for which the Nationalists stood were conceded.

[17] Swadeshi means the cult of home industries, *i. e.*, the use of the articles made in the country.

In the Congress camp, the younger generation had met in open conference to discuss their future programme. It was then that Mr. Tilak gave out the idea of passive resistance. No formal resolutions were passed, but the better mind of the people present decided to inaugurate an era of self-help and self-reliance based on an active boycott of government service and of the semi-government institutions.

Object of the Passive Resistance Movement. The object was two-fold. (1). To destroy the hypnotism that had caused the people and the country to have faith not only in the omnipotence of their rulers, but also in their altruism. In the words of one of the leaders of the Nationalist thought (Babu B. C. Pal,[18] "The Spirit of Indian Nationalism," page 42), the people had been hypnotised to believe in the altruism of their foreign rulers:

"Untrained in the crooked ways of civilised diplomacy, they had believed what their rulers had said, either of themselves or of their subjects, as gospel truth. They had been told that the people of India were unfitted to manage their own affairs, and they believed it to be true. They had been told that the people were weak and the Government was strong. They had been told that India stood on a lower plane of humanity and England's mission was to civilise 'the semi-barbarous native.' The Nationalist school took it upon themselves to expose the hollowness of all these pretensions. They commenced to make what are called counter-passes in

[18] An eminent Bengalee writer.

BAL GANGA DHAR TILAK

hypnotism, and at once awoke the people to a sense of their own strength, an appreciation of their own culture."

In the second place, the object was to create a passionate love of liberty, accompanied by a spirit of sacrifice and readiness to suffer for the cause of the country. This was to be done more by example than precept. What the programme was may better be stated in the words of the leader whom we have quoted above:

"Boycott both economic and political, boycott of foreign and especially British goods, and of all honorary associations with the administration, national education implying a withdrawal of the youths of the nation from the officialised universities and government-controlled schools and colleges, and training them up in institutions conducted on *national* lines subject to *national* control and calculated to help the realisation of the *national* destiny, national civic volunteering, aiming at imparting a healthy civic training to the people by the voluntary assumption of as much of the civic duties, at present discharged by official or semi-official agencies, as could be done without any violation of the existing laws of the country,— duties, for instance, in regard to rural sanitation, economic and medical relief, popular education, preventive police duties, regulation of fair and pilgrim gathering,— settlement of civil and non-cognisable, criminal disputes by means of arbitration committees:—these were the proclaimed methods of the Nationalist school."

As to the objects of this scheme, we will again quote the same writer:

"The evident object was to create in the first place a strong civic sentiment in the people with the help of co-operative organisations for the furtherance of the common good, and thus to train them gradually for the larger and heavier responsibilities of free citizenship, and in the next place, to cover the whole country with a net-work of active, political organisations which would place the leaders in direct and living touch with the people, and enable them to bring, from time to time, the irresistible pressure of organised public opinion to bear upon the Government, helping thereby the gradual expansion of popular rights."

Now it should be noted here in passing, that with the exception of boycott and volunteering, every other item in the above propaganda had been more or less tried and with varying success in all parts of the country, but more particularly in the Punjab and Maharashtra before this. The Deccan education Society and the Poona Fergusson College were the offshoots of the desire to further the cause of education by self-imposed sacrifices, with the underlying motives of quickening the patriotic impulse and the Nationalist spirit. Similarly Swadeshi, co-operative organisations, and private arbitration courts had been thought of and tried. The motives underlying these attempts were absolutely patriotic, combining an element of philanthropy in them. The private colleges in Bengal, started by Vidyasagar and others, were also due to the same impulse, and so was the

Pachaipiya College at Madras. Bombay had its own schemes and was ahead of the rest of India in purely Indian industrial and trade organisations. Similarly in the Punjab the idea of swadeshi had been started as early as 1877. The motives were economic and patriotic. The idea of national education had found expression in the D. A. V. (Dayanand Anglo-Vedic) College, and that of national co-operative organisations in the "Punjab National Bank," the "Bharat Insurance Company" and other joint stock concerns. Religious and philanthropic motives had brought into existence the Hindu orphan movement, the famine relief movement, and so on. A little volunteering had also been attempted in connection with the famine relief movement and the Kangra earthquake relief movement. Long before 1905, the Punjab had a network of privately organised, privately financed, unaided schools and other charitable institutions, over which the Government had little effective control. Patriotism and philanthropy were the underlying motives of these institutions, but *not politics*.[19]

The ruling bureaucracy did not quite like these activities, but they could not suppress them. Individual officers sometimes sympathised and even helped these movements. So far Bengal had been rather backward in the matter of national development on these lines. So, when Lord Curzon proclaimed the partition of Bengal, attacked the

[19] Moreover the keynote of these organisations was association and co-operation with Government, and not independent self-assertion.

veracity of the orientals in his Calcutta University convocation speech, and on other occasions called them cowards, windbags, unpractical talkers, and mere frothy patriots, the Bengalees awoke to a consciousness of their weaknesses, and resolved to revenge themselves upon Lord Curzon, and prove to the world at large that Lord Curzon was a liar. What followed may be briefly stated in a separate chapter.

CHAPTER IV

THE FIRST YEARS OF THE NATIONALIST MOVEMENT

Partition of Bengal. It was on the 16th of October, 1905, that the old Province of Bengal was partitioned by Lord Curzon. On that day "immense numbers of people in the two divisions of the partitioned province abstained from lighting their kitchen fire, went about barefooted, performed ceremonial baths in rivers or sacred tanks,[1] and tied on one another's wrist the sacred *rakhi,* a piece of silk or cotton thread, as a symbol of fraternal or national unity." On the 7th of August, 1905, the leaders of Bengal, in public meeting assembled, in the Calcutta Town Hall, under the presidency of Maharaja Mannidra Chandra Nundy of Cossimbazar,[2] had already declared "a general boycott of British goods as a practical protest against the proposed partition."

Boycott of British Goods. The original idea was to resort to boycott as a temporary measure, and therefore in the pledges drawn up in the early days, a time limit was put in. The boycott was to last until "the partition was withdrawn." In the words

[1] These are signs of mourning in India.
[2] An eminent nobleman and landlord of Bengal.

of a Bengalee politician, the idea was to cause pecuniary loss to the British manufacturer and thus enlist his sympathy and help for the purpose of getting the measure cancelled. But it was soon discovered that the boycott might be an effective economic weapon, to be used as a measure of protection against the economic exploitation of the country by the foreigner.

To quote the same writer, "The pledges sent from Calcutta came back, duly signed by large numbers of people, but with the conditional sentence, 'until Partition is withdrawn,' scored through. The boycott was a great success for some time. 'The Lucky Day' of October, 1905, on which generally a very large number of forward contracts in Manchester goods are made at Calcutta, passed without any business being done. Simultaneously with this decline in foreign goods, many indigenous industries began to revive. There was a boom in handlooms all over India. Provinces outside of Bengal did not adopt a policy of active boycott, but the cry of Swadeshi [3] was taken up by all the country, whereby a great impetus was given to indigenous manufacturers. The significance of the movement in Bengal, where it was rigorously pursued, lay in the fact that prince and peasant, capitalist and labourer, literate and illiterate, educated and uneducated, all joined hands." For some time the boycott was so effective that *The Englishman,* an Anglo-Indian newspaper published in Calcutta, declared: "It is absolutely true that Calcutta ware-

[3] India made goods.

houses are full of fabrics that can not be sold. In the earlier days of the boycott it was the fashion to assert that depression in piece goods trade was due to this or the other economic cause.

"Many prominent Marwari[4] Firms have been absolutely ruined and a number of the biggest European import houses have had either to close down their piece goods branch or to put up with a very small business, where they previously had a large one. As for stocks in warehouses, they tend to grow larger, as Marwari and Indian buyers who had given forward orders, now state that they can not afford to take delivery. These facts are now so well known that it is idle to attempt to hide them. Indeed the time has come when all injuries inflicted on trade by boycott should be made fully known. There is no question of encouraging the boycotters, as they need no encouragement. But there is the question of thoroughly awakening the public at home and the Government of India to the fact that in boycott the enemies of the Ráj have found a most effective weapon for injuring British interests in the country."

The triumph of the boycotters was testified to by the following remarks of *The Englishman,* with which the article ended: "The question however is, what is the Government going to do about it? *Boycott must not be acquiesced in, or it will more surely ruin British connection with India than an armed revolution.*" [The italics are ours.]

[4] Wholesale piece goods merchants belonging to Upper India are known in Calcutta by that name.

Government's Reply. In reply to this move on the part of the Bengalee leaders,— a move in which all Bengal was united, including the present moderates,— the Government started a crusade against the students whom the boycotters had enlisted in their service. The bureaucracy thought that the more active part of the propaganda was carried on by them. According to Mr. B. C. Pal, "the success of the boycott, especially in the earlier stages before the sentiment had time to settle down into the conscience and consciousness of the people, depended almost entirely upon picketing." Mr. Pal assures us that "their method was uniformly intellectual and moral," and that "there was no intimidation, no violence, no appeal to physical fear, none of the things that characterise picketing among the robuster people of the West."

The British, of course, do not accept this statement as true. But whatever its nature, the Government did not like picketing. They thought they could not stand by and let a movement of that kind gain strength. "Their first move was to make it penal for the young student population to participate in any way in the nationalist activities. Students who attended public meetings were threatened with various punishments to the extent even of expulsion from school, college, or university."

The Second Move of the Bengalees: The National University. The Bengalee leaders then put their heads together and resolved to start a National University, wherein education would be given independent of government control. The educational policy of Lord Curzon had already set people to thinking along that line. The measures now adopted to strike at the boycott movement by punishing the students who participated therein "accentuated the need and called forth actual measures to meet it." This movement also, like the boycott, met the universal support of United Bengal. The actual leadership of it fell on Sir Gurdas Bannerjea, late Judge of the Calcutta High Court, who had been vice-chancellor of the Calcutta University for some time and whose loyalty and moderation had never been questioned by friend or foe. Besides, he had sat on the University Commission appointed by Lord Curzon and had written a note of dissent from the policy recommended by the majority of its members. "Under his guidance, the Bengal Council of National Education proposed to work, independent of, but by no means in opposition to, the Government Education Department. And this independent activity was justified on the ground that the education hitherto imparted under official supervision lacked a vital reference to the thoughts, the sentiments, the traditions, the religions, and even the outer physical and biological environments of the people. The object of the new movement was to organise a thoroughly national system of education, both scientific and literary, as well as technical, on *national lines* and under *national control.*"

Besides making an ample provision for literary, scientific, and technical education, the National Council of Education at once reduced English to the status of a secondary language, the first place being given to Bengalee and Sanskrit, and in the case of Mohammedans to Urdu, Persian, and Arabic.

The National Education Movement in Bengal was in no way an anti-government movement. Though it owed its "initiation to the threats of the Government to close the doors of the official schools and colleges and universities against those who would take any part in, even to the extent of simply attending, any political meeting or demonstration, the National Education Movement in Bengal sought to avoid all open causes of friction with the authorities and proposed to work *independent of,* but not in *opposition to,* the Government. Political in its origin, it tried to avoid all conflicts with the authorities by assuming an absolutely non-political attitude."

Arabinda Ghosh. To this movement, Indian Nationalism owes the emerging into prominence of a quiet, unostentatious, young Hindu, who was till then comparatively obscure, holding his soul in patience and waiting for opportunities to send currents of the greatest strength into the nation's system. He was gathering energy. His name was Arabinda Ghosh. Arabinda had received first class education in England. The headmaster of the school, where he studied before joining the university, is reported to have said that during the 25 to 30 years he had been in charge of the school, Arabinda Ghosh was by far the most richly endowed in intellectual capacity of any of the students that had come under his charge.

At Cambridge he distinguished himself in European classics and took first class honours. He

ARABINDA GHOSH

passed the Indian Civil Service examinations with credit, but failed in the test for horsemanship. Never did a failure prove more a blessing than in his case.

He was in the service of His Highness, the Maharaja of Baroda,[5] drawing a salary of about 500 pounds sterling, when his country's call came to him. He listened to it readily, gave up his post and agreed to be the principal of the National College on ten pounds a month. We are told by one who worked with him for some time that he did not support the "declaration of the National Council of Education" about their non-political attitude. He could not appreciate this needless dread, as they thought, of offending official susceptibilities. He, however, accepted the verdict of the majority and began his work. But his position as "the nominal head of the National College, controlled by men" who "differed from him in their political views and opinions, became almost from the very beginning anomalous." This was rather unfortunate. Arabinda Ghosh had received the best modern education that any man of his country and generation could expect to have. He had for some years been a teacher of youth in Baroda and had acquired considerable experience in his art. He had clearly realised the spirit and actualities of the life of his nation, and knew how the most advanced principles of pedagogy could be successfully worked into a thoroughly national system of education in India. He knew that the foundations of national independence and national great-

[5] A ruling chief in the Bombay Presidency.

ness must be laid in a strong and advanced system of national education. He had a political ideal, no doubt; but politics meant to him much more than is ordinarily understood by the term. It was not a game of expediency, but a "school of human character" which acted and reacted on the life of the nation. "Education could no more be divorced from politics," in his opinion, "than it could be divorced from religion and morals. Any system of education that helps such isolation and division between the various organic relations of life is mediæval and not modern." [6]

The monied leaders of the National Council of Education movement, however, could not accept Arabinda's principles. "They were not free from the fear of possible official opposition, which, if once aroused, would make their work, they thought, absolutely impossible. They had a real dread of the bureaucracy" whom they were not prepared to defy. Experience has shown that they were quite mistaken if they thought they could develop their scheme of education without rousing the fears and the bitterest opposition of the bureaucracy, even after declaring the non-political character of their scheme.

Never before in the history of the human race was it so well realised as now that the school is the nursery of the man and the citizen. Lord Curzon realised it in full and it was his aim to curtail or, if possible, crush the nationalist influences in the

[6] In my opinion there has never been any time in human history when religion and morals were successfully divorced from politics, either in Ancient India or anywhere else.

schools and colleges managed and conducted by Indian agencies. It was his desire to introduce the English element in all these institutions and to put them under English control. He had invited European missionaries to the Secret Educational Conference at Simla, but not a single Indian, Hindu or Mohammedan. He could not trust them (*i. e.,* the Indians) with his ideas. Hence the need of secrecy. The National Council of Education was supposed to be working against the spirit of his policy. He was gone, but the bureaucracy who were identified with his wishes, views and schemes, were there. It was impossible that they would let the Bengalees, whoever they might be, build up a system of education and a network of educational institutions, that not only would owe nothing to the Government but were also to be quite free of official or English control and of English influence.

Then, the very circumstances under which the National College was born and the National Schools affiliated to it were opened, gave them a political character. The Government and the bureaucracy were opposed to the students taking any part in the boycott movement; the Bengalee leaders wanted them to do so, and hence the National College and the National Schools. It was an open challenge — a revolt. Arabinda Ghosh was identified with this revolt, and with him were associated a whole group of powerful writers and speakers, all men of high individuality and lofty ideals and of pure character. They accepted the decision of the majority about the non-political character of the college, but no one could deprive them of the use of their pen and tongue. Any attempt to do that might have been fatal to the scheme. They started journals and preached the gospel of political and economic and educational independence in the clearest language. They were all men of education and knew their history well. They fully realised what the consequences were likely to be, and they were prepared for it. They were prepared to suffer for their propaganda, but they were not yet prepared for violence.

The Nationalist Press. They started a number of papers in Bengalee and also in English, in which they gave their ideas to the people. The *Sandhya* and the *Bande Mátaran,* as two of the new papers were called, became their classrooms. In a few months the face and the spirit of Bengal was changed. The press, the pulpit, the platform, the writers of prose and poetry, composers of music and playwrights, all were filled with the spirit of nationalism. Bande Mataram (Hail Motherland) was the cry of the day. It was chanted in schools, in colleges, in streets, in houses, in public squares, almost everywhere. Even the government offices and the compounds of the private residences of European officials resounded with it.

Sabhas and *Samitis* and *Akharas* [7] leaped into existence by hundreds, where the Bengalee young men began to take lessons in fencing and other games. This was their reply to those who taunted them as cowards; for the famous, or rather infamous, re-

[7] Societies, Associations and Gymnasiums.

marks of Macaulay about Bengalees were often hurled at their heads by the Anglo-Indians, or new language was used to express the same thoughts.

The boycott had created an unheard of situation in some of the districts in Eastern Bengal. In one district — Barisal — the Superintendent of Police and the Collector had both failed to be able to buy a piece of Manchester shirting for one of their friends, as no trader would sell it except by permission of the gentleman who was the leader of the boycotters. This leader happened to be a man who had made his influence by his character and by service. He was, so to say, the uncrowned king of his district. That was a crusher to the bureaucracy. No foreign bureaucracy could tolerate it. Sir William Bamfylde Fuller, on whom had fallen the first Lieutenant Governorship of Eastern Bengal, was bewildered by the strength of the movement and the new character which the Bengalees were developing. The people refused to show him the customary honours. Even the presence of the Lieutenant Governor in the town did not prevent the people from giving ovations to anti-partition propagandists and making anti-partition demonstrations. At one place it is said that even the railway porters refused to touch his baggage, which had to be carried by police constables. This was more than he could bear.

Military Measures against Boycotters. After consultation with Lord Curzon, he resolved to use force. The first step taken was the despatch of a hundred Gurkha troops to Barisal, followed by a demand for the withdrawal of a circular issued by the local leaders advising the people of the legality of a peaceful boycott of British goods. It was evident that a refusal meant a physical conflict, which the leaders were yet anxious to avoid. So the leaders decided to withdraw and the governor was mollified. The Gurkhas are said to have committed numerous outrages on the people, but the leaders kept the latter under control, as they did not want the Government to get a handle to crush the movement by force.

In April, 1906, the Provincial Conference, which was attended by the most prominent leaders of the two Bengals, was broken up by order of the Magistrate "almost at the point of the bayonet." A procession of some 800 or 900 delegates from the different districts of the two provinces, "including almost every prominent leader in the country, was dispersed by the police, who made a free use of their quarterstaffs and broke more than one head under the very eyes of the District Superintendent of Police." The people, however, did not retaliate. So far, they were determined not to use force even against force. With every display of force on the side of the Government, the nationalist movement gained ground in popularity and in strength, until the masses, the women and children, all were saturated with it.

This was the birth of a new life in Bengal, which found its reflection in every phase of public activity, religious, social, economic, educational, or political. What was done in Bengal found its echo in the rest of the country. So far the Nationalist party was united. The elder people, who had been born and bred and had lived in a different atmosphere, were not in full accord with the younger party and remonstrated with the latter, when they indulged in intemperate language. Some people in other provinces did not quite approve of the wholesale boycott, inaugurated and declared by the Bengalees, but otherwise the nation was united, and the best mind of the nation was rather gratified at the turn things had taken.

Lord Minto. With the advent of Lord Minto (in 1905), however, things began to assume a different shape. The first serious difference in the Nationalist party occurred over the presidentship of the Indian National Congress at Calcutta in 1906, but an actual split was avoided by a clever and diplomatic move of the leaders of the new moderate party, who obtained the consent of Mr. Dadabhai Naoroji[8] to accept the presidentship, if offered to him. The Congress session of 1906 was rather an uproarious session, but eventually the spirit of compromise and conciliation prevailed and the so-called extremists practically gained all their points so far as the principle of them was concerned.

But it was clear, even to a superficial observer, that a split was inevitable; Lord Minto had succeeded Lord Curzon as Viceroy, and a visible change was coming in the policy of the Government. Lord Curzon was for a policy of repression; Minto

[8] A leader universally respected and loved by all classes of people throughout India. See frontispiece.

inaugurated a reign of conciliation with repression. The movement might have succumbed if the Government had been courageous enough to annul or modify the Partition of Bengal, as they subsequently did in 1912. But that was not to be. On that point the Government would not yield, though otherwise they were in favour of making concessions.

Indian Press Gagged. The years 1905, 1906, and 1907 were years of passive resistance. The nationalists indulged in strong language, carried on a vigorous anti-British propaganda by means of the press and the platform, used their pen and tongue rather freely, but did not think of using force. Editor after editor, and publisher after publisher was sent to prison without any diminution of the campaign. The years 1906 and 1907 saw a regular "tug of war" between the Government on the one side and the nationalists on the other. A large number of prosecutions were launched against the members of the press in Bengal and Bombay, Punjab and the United Provinces, Madras and the Central Provinces, and many persons were sentenced to long terms of imprisonment. A complete boycott, economic, political and social, was openly preached, and picketing was again resorted to. Some of the judicial trials were only farcical, the judges being influenced by political considerations, and convictions and sentences being foregone conclusions. Yet such was the people's regard for law, that so long as the procedure of an open trial was not attacked, they did not think of employing

From a painting by Mrs. Rieber, Berkeley, Cal.

LAJPAT RAI

force for purposes of revenge. Even ill-treatment, either in lock-ups, during trial, or in prisons, after conviction, failed to incite the people to force. Political prisoners were applauded, glorified, and otherwise supported and backed, but no thought of revenge entered anybody's head.

Deportation of Lajpat Rai. The sudden deportation of Lajpat Rai, however, in May, 1907, changed the whole current of thought and action. The nationalists concluded that the movement for passive resistance required to be supported by secret propaganda as well as the use of force against force. In the words of the Honourable Mr. G. K. Gokhale, in a speech delivered in the Council of the Governor General after the deportation of Lajpat Rai, the latter was a religious, social, and educational reformer and was loved and respected by large classes of his countrymen all over the country. He was one of the persons whom the extreme Nationalists claimed as their own, whom the moderate Nationalists also respected, and whom the populace "liked for his philanthropic and educational activities." The sudden capture of this man, without trial, without charge, and without notice, drove the young Nationalists to frenzy.[9] Even the sober and the thoughtful among the Nationalists were in despair.

The Anglo-Indian press all over the country, however, was in jubilation. The leading semi-official daily published at Lahore, the headquarters

[9] See Mr. H. W. Nevinson's New Spirit in India, p. 295; also pp. 133, 233, etc.; see also Mr. J. Ramsay Macdonald's Awakening of India.

of Lajpat Rai, described him as the leader of a deep-laid revolutionary movement, every detail of which passed through his fingers. He was said to have a following of "100,000 desperadoes." *The Englishman*, at Calcutta, charged him with having tampered with the loyalty of the Indian army, and having incited the King of Afghanistan to invade India. As a result of adding, as they did, insult to the injury of deportation, the country was ablaze with indignation. The step was condemned by the unanimous voice of the people. All differences of opinion were forgotten and the whole country joined in protest. The extreme wing of the nationalists, however, decided to take the next step. They decided to use force and began to think of bomb and revolver and of a guerilla warfare against the established despotism. The older people, though they sympathised, would not agree to take any part in the movement using physical force, nor would they give their sanction to such a course.

It is possible that some sort of secret organisation existed in Bengal in 1906, but force did not enter into their programme till after May, 1907, i. e., until after the deportation of Lajpat Rai. The deportation decided them. Yet the first shot was not fired until December, 1907, and the first bomb was not thrown until April or May, 1908. The split [10] at Surat in December, 1907, irrevocably divided the Nationalists into two parties, and confirmed the younger party in their programme of force. The

[10] For an account of this split see H. W. Nevinson's New Spirit in India, Chap. XIII.

extremists saw the hand of the Government in the split. Within a few months almost all the leaders were seized and thrown into prison. At Surat, Lajpat Rai, having thrown in his lot with the moderates, was for a time left alone, but Bal Gânga Dhar Tilak, the Mahratta leader, was prosecuted and sentenced to six years' transportation. Arabinda Ghosh was also seized and prosecuted for conspiracy to wage war against the King, though he was afterwards acquitted for want of evidence. Bepin Chandra Pal was also seized and sentenced to six months' imprisonment; Chidambaran Pillai, a Madras leader, to six years; a Mohammedan leader of the United Provinces, Abul Hasan Hasrat Mohani, to one year. In December, 1908, nine of the Bengal leaders were seized in their homes and imprisoned by an administrative order without trial and without charge.

Disaffection Driven Underground. These persecutions and sentences exasperated the younger party and drove disaffection underground. Undaunted by the loss of leaders, they continued their propaganda and made several attempts on the lives of high officials. The life of the Lieutenant Governor of Bengal was attempted no less than three times, once in open daylight, when he was presiding at a certain state function. The life of the viceroy, Lord Minto, was also attempted, at Ahmedabad. The political secretary of Lord Morley, then Secretary of State, was shot in London; a collector was murdered at Nasik, and many other "outrages" were committed. Publications suppressed and condemned were published and circulated secretly; arms were smuggled and stolen; and attempts were made to wreck railways and otherwise terrorise the Government. Throughout the year 1908 and 1909 the movement was kept up at high pressure. Then in 1910 there was a comparative lull, though the revolutionary activities did come up to the surface occasionally.

The year 1911 was perhaps the dullest year from the revolutionary point of view. That was the year of the King's visit to India. The King modified the Partition of Bengal and ordered the transfer of the capital to Delhi. For a time there was a great rejoicing in the country, not so much because the Partition had been annulled, but because it was a virtual triumph of the Nationalist agitation.

Lord Hardinge Bombed. In December, 1912, again, the revolutionary party gave conclusive evidence of their existence and strength. A bomb was thrown at Lord Hardinge, the Viceroy, when he was passing in procession midst thousands of troops and hundreds of thousands of spectators, making his first state entry into the new capital of British India, the Delhi of the Moguls. Lord Hardinge was wounded, members of his entourage killed and the procession broken up. The culprit escaped, and in spite of offers of huge rewards [11] and unprecedented police activity has remained undetected up to the present time. This is considered to be

[11] A reward of one hundred thousand Rupees equal to 33,000 dollars was offered for information leading to the arrest of the culprit or culprits.

the supreme achievement of the revolutionaries. Throughout 1913 and 1914 the revolutionaries were active, and the scanty news that has filtered out from India during the war gives ample reason to think that they are very active now.

Within the last seven or eight years, the Government has tried every form of repression, and has also planned a programme of partial reconciliation, but they have so far failed to crush the extreme wing of the Nationalist party, the wing that believes in force and that has taken to all the methods of guerilla warfare against a foreign government based on force.

The country is in such circumstances now that every step which the Government takes to repress and crush the movement or to punish the offenders, strengthens the spirit of revolt, adds to the volume and intensity of the desire for revenge, adds to the number of those who are prepared to suffer or even die for the cause. From the classes, the movement has spread to the masses; from the non-fighting masses it is now gaining ground and winning adherents among the fighting classes. In 1907 the charge of tampering with the army, laid at the door of Lajpat Rai, was ridiculous. Perhaps there was a certain amount of disaffection among the Punjab regiments due to the Agrarian legislation undertaken by the Punjab Government, which deeply and detrimentally affected the classes from which the army was recruited. When the legislation objected to was vetoed, that cause of disaffection was removed; but since then fresh causes have affected at least certain sections of the army also, so that it cannot be said that the whole army is free from disaffection. The riot at Singapore, caused by the revolt of one of the Indian regiments stationed there, and certain happenings in the Punjab, amply prove this.

CHAPTER V

TYPES OF NATIONALISTS

We will now see how many types of Nationalists there are in India. From what follows in the chapter, the reader should not conclude that the Indian Nationalists are disunited. So far as the goal is concerned there is practical unanimity in all ranks. Even those who stand for complete independence would be glad to have self-government within the Empire, if that were promised in the near future. As to methods, there is the usual cleavage to be found in all struggles for freedom in all countries. One party stands for the use of physical force, the other for peaceful means. The Indian Nationalists, too, are divided into two parties, the physical force party and the moderate party. The following account of the types is intended to show the different lines of their thinking. Complete unanimity in principles and methods can only be expected of a collection of machine-made clogs of wood.

The Extremists. (1) To take up the extremists first: There are some who do not recognise the British Government at all. They think that the Government of the British in India is founded on force and fraud. They have therefore no scruples to use force as well as fraud against the Government. In their eyes every one who is helping the Government in India either by accepting their service or otherwise by willing co-operation, abets the crime of which the Britishers are guilty. They do not recognise British laws nor their courts. They have no respect or use for either. They believe that their nationalism gives them the right of removing every one who stands in the way of their propaganda, whether by force or fraud. In their heart of hearts they are against every one who supports the British Government in India, but in the prosecution of their object they do not desire to strike at all of them. But if need be they are prepared to strike at any one. They have declared war against the British Government. Their leaders have assumed the right of passing sentences against those who are of the enemy. They judge and deal severely with those whom they think guilty of treason against them. They also consider themselves entitled to collect taxes as they call them, and make impositions on people in India. Acting on the principle that the safety of the state is the first consideration for all those who form the state, and that in case of necessity the state has a right to use the property of every private individual who is included in the body politic, they are prepared to exact their impositions by force. The fact that the British Government is the enemy against whom they have declared war, gives them the right to loot British treasuries and injure their property wherever and whenever they can.

The other principle stated above justifies in their

eyes the taking by force of the property or wealth of those who would not give it willingly or voluntarily for the safety of the state as conceived by them. Hence the "dacoities."

A few Nihilists. The men engaged in those dacoities are of two kinds: There are those who have no moral or religious scruples. They are "*nihilists.*" But their number is exceedingly small. They are not immoral people. For their own self or for private persons, they would not do anything which in any way contravenes the prevailing code of morality; they would neither steal nor rob, nor kill nor injure any person. But for the purpose of their movement they would do anything. Their number however is, as we said above, exceedingly small. Then there are those who are extremely religious and spiritual. Some of them are the followers of the "*Kali*"[1] cult as it is understood in Bengal; others are Vedantists. There are some who are deists or theists.

Religious Extremists. In every case, however, they believe that the British are the enemies of their Motherland and also of their religion. They would not touch one hair of any one simply because that person belonged to a religion different from theirs; but they would not scruple to kill any one who interferes with their religion. They believe that they owe their lives to the Motherland, whom they worship as the means of enabling them to be worthy of the worship of the Supreme Mother of the Universe.

[1] Name of a religious sect. See Pratts' India and Its Faiths, p. 13.

We will once more quote Mr. Pal [2] to explain what we mean, or rather how he puts the idea:

The Mother Worshippers. "The so-called idolatry of Hinduism," he says, "is also passing through a mighty transfiguration. The process started really with Bankim Chandra,[3] who interpreted the most popular of the Hindu goddesses as symbolic of the different stages of national evolution. *Jagatdhatri* — riding a lion which has the prostrate body of an elephant under its paw, represented the motherland in the early jungle-clearing stage. This is, says Bankim Chandra, the mother as she was. *Kali,* the grim goddess, dark and naked, bearing a garland of human heads around her neck,— heads from which blood is dripping,— and dancing on the prostrate form of Shiva, the God — this, says Bankim Chandra, is the mother as she is, dark, because ignorant of herself; the heads with dripping blood are those of her own children, destroyed by famine and pestilence; the jackals [4] licking these drippings are the symbol of desolation and decadence of social life, and the prostrate form of Shiva means that she is trampling her own God under her feet. *Durga,* the ten-headed goddess, armed with swords and spears in some hands, holding wheat-sheaves in some, offering courage and peace with others, riding a lion, fighting with demons; with Sarasvati, or the goddess of Knowledge and Arts, supported by

[2] The Spirit of Indian Nationalism, by Mr. B. C. Pal. p. 36.

[3] A great Bengalee writer of fiction who composed the well-known nationalist song, "Bande Mataram" or Hail Motherland.

[4] Or the foreign exploiters.

Ganapati, the god of Wisdom, on her one side, and Lakshmi, the goddess of Wealth, protected by Kartikeya, the leader of the Heavenly army, on the other side — this, says Bankim Chandra, is the mother as she will be. This interpretation of the old images of gods and goddesses has imparted a new meaning to the current ceremonialism of the country, and multitudes, while worshipping either *Jagatdhatri,* or *Kali,* or *Durga,* accost them with devotion and enthusiasm, with the inspiring cry of Bande Mataram. All these are the popular objects of worship of the Indian Hindus, especially in Bengal. And the transfiguration of these symbols is at once the cause and the evidence of the depth and the strength of the present movement. This wonderful transfiguration of the old gods and goddesses is carrying the message of new nationalism to the women and the masses of the country."

Vedantists. "Behind this mighty transfiguration of the old religious ideas and symbols of the country stands, however, a new philosophy of life. Strictly speaking, it is not a new philosophy either, but rather a somewhat new application of the dominant philosophical speculations of the race. Behind the new nationalism in India stands the old Vedantism of the Hindus. This ancient Indian philosophy, divided into many schools, has one general idea running through it from end to end. It is the idea of the essential unity of man and God. According to this philosophy, Substance is one though expressed through many forms. Reality is one though appearances are multitudinous. Matter, in the eye of this philosophy, is not material, but essentially spiritual, the thought of God concretised. Man is the spirit of God incarnated. The meaning of cosmic evolution is to be found, not in itself, but in the thought of the Absolute. It is, to adopt the Hegelian dictum, the movement of the Self away from itself, to return to itself, to be itself. The Absolute, or Brahman, is the beginning, the middle, and the end of this evolutionary process. He is the Regulative idea. He is cosmic evolution. He is progressively revealing himself through the world process. In man, the Divine idea, or the Logos, comes slowly to consciousness of itself. The end of human evolution is the fullest realisation of man's unity with God. Long, especially in what may be called the middle ages in India, this essential unity between God and man was sought to be realised through metaphysical abstractions, by negation of the social and civic life. There was an undue emphasis on the Subjective and the Universal to the neglect of the realities (however relative they might be) of the Objective and the Particular. Protests had, however, been made from time to time against these monkish abstractions, but in spite of these abstractions the dominant note continued to be that of Abstract Monism. Neo-Vedantism, which forms the very soul and essence of what may be called Neo-Hinduism, has been seeking to realise the old spiritual ideals of the race, not through monkish negations or mediæval abstractions, but by the idealisation and the spiritualisation of the concrete contents and actual relations of life. It demands, consequently, a social, an economic, and a political reconstruction, such as will be helpful to the highest spiritual life of every individual member of the community. The spiritual note of the present Nationalist Movement in India is entirely derived from this Vedantic thought.

"Under the influence of this Neo-Vedantism, associated to a large extent with the name of the late Swami Vivekananda, there has been at work a slow and silent process of the liberalisation of the old social ideas. The old bigotry that anathematised the least deviation from the rules of caste, or the authority of custom, is openly giving way to a spirit of new tolerance. The imperious necessities of national struggle and national life are slowly breaking down, except in purely ceremonial affairs, the old restrictions of caste. In the new movement, old and orthodox Brahmins are rendering open obeisance to the heterodox and non-Brahmin teachers. There is an evident anxiety to discover spiritual and traditional authority for even the outrages that some of these have committed against the old social and sacerdotal order. And where no such authority could be found, their personal freedom of thought and action is being condoned on the principle that those who are to be the saviours of their nation stand, like the mendicant and the holy man, above all law. And all this is a proof of the strange hold that the new nationalist propaganda has got on the real mind and soul of the people."

To these two classes, the Mother worshippers, and the Vedantists, belong the great bulk of the Bengal Nationalists. They are neither "nihilists" nor "anarchists." They are patriots who have raised their patriotism to the pitch of a religion. Their religion remarkably fits in with their patriotism and makes the latter indescribably intense and alive. Their whole life is permeated with it. They realise their "duty" every moment of their life and they are prepared to do anything and take any and every risk in the performance of that duty. They live on little; their food is abstemious; they scrupulously avoid liquor; they clothe themselves scantily; luxury they do not know. They can fast for days and go without sleep for days. Generally they are men of their word, men of honour, imbued with a strong idea of self-respect, true to their vows; men who are not swayed by lust or passion.

To this class belonged most of the Maniktolah party, Barendra and his friends. But it is evident that there are some theists among them, *i. e.*, theists in the Western sense of the term. The man who shot Gossain, the first *approver*[5] in Bengal, was a

[5] It was in the first half of the year 1908 that the first bomb was thrown at Muzaffarpur, Behar. It was meant for a Magistrate who had been passing sentences of whipping on nationalist youths, but by mistake it struck a quite innocent person. The investigation of this case resulted in the discovery of a big conspiracy. The trial of this conspiracy is known by the name "Maniktolah Bomb Case" from the fact that the headquarters of this conspiracy were alleged to have been in the Maniktolah gardens, Calcutta. One of the conspirators Narendra Nath Gossain became an approver. After the case had been committed for trial before the Sessions Court and when the approver and the accused were both lodged in jail at Alipore, one of the leaders of the conspiracy shot the approver dead with a rifle which had been smuggled into the jail premises by their friends.

HAR DAYAL

Brahmo (member of the Brahmo Samaj). They have some Mohammedans and some Christians, too, among them. *Brahm Bhandu Bandhopadhyai*[6] was a Christian at one time. These people have followers and adherents throughout India, in the Punjab, in the United Provinces, in Maharastra, in Gujrat, in Behar, in Rajputana, even in Madras.

Advocates of Organised Rebellion. (2) Next in order come those who differ from the first in so far as they do not believe in individual murders or dacoities. For traitors and approvers even they have no mercy, but they would not murder individual British officers or Indians in the service of the Government; nor would they rob private persons. They are for organised rebellion, for tampering with the army, for raising the standard of revolt, and for carrying on a guerilla war. For the purposes of this rebellion or war they may do and will do anything that is necessary to be done; but otherwise they would neither murder nor loot.

Har Dayal. To this class, I think, belongs Har Dayal. It is very interesting to note the development of this man. He comes from a Kayastha family of Delhi and received his education in a mission school and a mission college under Christian influence. He was a member of the Young Men's Christian Association when he graduated. Then he came to Lahore and joined the government college there, as a stipend holder, where he took his Master of Arts degree in 1903, standing at the top of the list. His subject was " English language and litera-

[6] A great Nationalist leader of Bengal, now dead.

ture" and so thorough was his mastery of the language that in some papers he obtained full marks. He continued there for another year and took his M.A. degree a second time in History. All this time he was a cosmopolitan, more of a Brahmo than a Hindu or a Nationalist. Then he left for England, having secured a Government of India scholarship, and joined the St. John's College at Oxford. It is needless to say that even here he maintained his reputation for brilliant scholarship, but what is remarkable is, that it was here that he became a Nationalist. He is a man of strong impulses. For him, to believe is to act. It appears that within a short time he developed ideas of a rather extreme type. He came to believe that the English were undermining Hindu character; that their educational policy and methods had been designed to destroy Hinduism and to perpetuate the political bondage of the Hindus, by destroying their social consciousness and their national individuality. He studied the history of the British rule and British institutions in India from original documents, parliamentary blue books and varied other sources, and came to the conclusion that the British were deliberately Anglicising the Indians with a view to destroying their nationalism and to impressing them with the inferiority of their institutions, so that they might value the British connection and become Britishers. He thought it wrong to study in their institutions, take their degrees, and otherwise benefit from anything which they did as rulers of India. As we have said above, for him to believe was to act. As soon as he formed the above opinions, he made up his mind to resign his stipend, give up his studies, and return to India, which he did towards the end of 1907. Even before he reached India, he gave up English dress and began to eschew all the peculiarities of English life. He took to Indian shoes, Indian cap, Indian Kurta (shirt), Indian Pajama (troùsers) and wrapped himself in an Indian shawl. He would not even mix with Mohammedans and Christians. For a time he was a strict Hindu in form, though not in religion. When his old master, Principal Rudra of the Delhi St. Stephen's College, called on him at Lahore, he would not shake hands with him nor offer him a seat on his mat, because he was a Christian (he had no chairs). His cult at that time was a wholesale and complete boycott of British government and British institutions. He aimed to establish an order of Hindu ascetics to preach his ideas and to spread his propaganda. With that view he collected about half a dozen young men about him, who, under his inspiration, left their studies as well as their homes and showed their readiness to do as he would wish them to do. He lived a life of purity and wanted others to do the same. At that time he did not believe in or preach violence. He discussed, argued, preached, and wrote for the press. His writings began to attract attention, and so did his activities, and it was feared that the Government would soon find some means of putting him out of the way. So he decided to leave the country, and in the beginning of the second half of the year 1908 left India for good. He went to England, with the idea of preaching his gospel among the Indian students in England. He stayed there for some time and found out that there was not much scope for his type of nationalism. He also feared that the British Government might arrest him. So he left England and for about two years travelled, to and fro, to find a place where he could live very cheaply and without fear of molestation from the British Government and carry on his propaganda. He was for over a year in France, where he came in contact with the best political thought of Europe. Here he made friends with Egyptian nationalists and Russian revolutionists. His knowledge of the French language was good. He could not only speak that language fluently, but could compose in it. He used to write occasionally for the French press. He can use the German language also. Eventually he came to America and settled here. The contributions that he made to the Indian press during the first year of his sojourn in the United States did not indicate any very great change in his views on Nationalism, but a year after he was quite a different man. His political nationalism remained the same, but his views on social questions, on morality, on Hindu literature and Hindu institutions, underwent a complete metamorphosis. He began to look down upon everything Hindu and developed a great admiration for Occidental ideas of freedom. There is, however, one thing about him that has stuck fast, and that is his hatred of British rule in India. His present cult is to dissuade Indians from engaging in any work except that of political propaganda. We are told by him (that was what he said to American journalists at the time of his arrest in San Francisco as an undesirable alien) that he is not an anarchist and that he does not advocate the use of bomb and of revolver for private murders or for the murders of individuals. We have no reason to disbelieve him. Nobody, however, knows what changes are yet to take place in his views. He is a quite uncertain item. He is an idealist of a strange type. He is simple in his life and apparently quite indifferent to the opinions of others about him. He does not court favour at the hands of any one and would go out of his way to help others. He is loved and respected by hundreds and thousands of his countrymen, including those who do not agree with his views or his propaganda or his programme. Even the late Mr. Gokhale admired him.

Hardayalism. Har Dayal is an advocate of open rebellion; he does not advocate the use of the bomb or the revolver for killing individuals, but he admires and glorifies those who have risked their lives using the same.[7]

Neither of these classes is prepared to make any compromise with the British. They stand for absolute independence; full *Swaraj.* They know, perhaps, that they have a very difficult task before them, but they have confidence in themselves and believe that the difficulties are not insuperable. They do not believe that in order to gain Swaraj, India

[7] One of his followers in San Francisco has told me that this description of him, viz., that he does not advocate the use of the bomb or the revolver is not correct.

should have more widespread education, or that social reform and social consolidation must precede political freedom. They consider that these are all fads, ideas with which the British have inoculated the Indians in order to keep them busy with non-political activities and to keep down their manhood. It is a part of the imperial game that the rulers should manage to fill the ruled with the idea of their own incompetence to manage their affairs, of their inability to unite, of many differences and divisions among them, and of their incapacity to win their freedom. These nationalists deprecate communal or sectional activities. They do not countenance the organisations engaged in religious and social reform. In their opinion all these so-called reform organisations are doing positive mischief in keeping the nation engaged in less important matters and in directing the nation's mind from the all important question of national freedom. They want to concentrate the nation's mind on this one point.

Political Freedom the First Condition of Life. According to them life in political bondage or in political subjection is a negation of life. Life signifies power and capacity to grow and progress. A slave, a bondsman, is not free to grow. His interests are always subordinate to those of his master. He must give the best in him to the service of the latter. His will must always be under his master's will, who is practically his conscience's keeper. No man can grow to the full stature of his manhood; no man can rise to the best in him; no man can make the best use of his faculties and opportunities; no man can develop either his body or his soul according to his liking, under these circumstances. Whatever he does, he does for his master, in his name and in his interest. The credit and the glory and the benefit of it, all accrue to him.[8] If this is true of an individual slave, it is equally true of a nation in political bondage.

As a proof of the truth of their statements, they point to the history and activities of the Indian National Congress. The Congress people ask for Universal Primary Education; the Government says no. They can not find money for it; "the country is not prepared for it; nor is it good for the people at large." If the masses are educated, they might become discontented and create trouble for the Government. The Congress wants a repeal of the Arms Act; the Government says no. The people might use the arms against the Government, and that is a calamity to be avoided. The Congress desires that Indians be enrolled as volunteers; the Government says no. It is not desirable to give military training to the Indians. They might use it against the Government. It is not desirable to have companies of volunteers composed of Indians only, as they might conspire against the reigning power. It is equally undesirable to force them on European and Eurasian companies against their wishes, as that would wound their social and imperial susceptibilities. The Congress politician wants to protect Indian industries;

[8] This is illustrated in Indian official life day in and day out. It is not a rare occurrence that the British heads of the Departments get credit for what has been achieved by the genius, intelligence and labour of their Indian subordinates.

the Government says no. That will injure Lancashire. The Congress wants more of technical education; the Government says, the country does not need it and they can not spare funds for it. The Congress wants national schools and national universities; the Government says no, "you may misuse them." The keynote of the situation is, that India must exist in the interests of England and Englishmen; or at any rate England and English politicians know what is good and useful for India, how much she should and how much she should not have; in what line she should advance and in what she should not. India and Indians have no right to think for themselves. Anything they think or decide to do must be tested by Englishmen according to their standards and in the way they think it is likely to further the interests of their empire.

These nationalists therefore maintain that the first condition of life,—life with respect and honour, life for profit and advantage, life for progress and advancement,—is political freedom. Life without that is no life. It is idle therefore to think of matters which are manifestations or developments or embellishments of life.

Education can only profit a living being. A human being instructed on the lines on which certain beasts or animals are instructed, can, like the latter, only respond to the calls of his master. The master wants them to salute; they salute. The master wants them to dance; they dance. The master wants them to do any other job for him; they do it. Their will and intellect are always subordinate to the master. Independent of the master, they have neither will nor intellect. Education under these circumstances, they maintain, is a degrading of human faculties, and a travesty. In their opinion it would be best for their people to remain uneducated, rather than be educated only for the benefit and use of their masters.

Similarly they think that all the schemes for social reform, for sectarian advancement, for commercial interests, are nothing more than so many devices for dividing the nation and keeping them engaged in never-ending internecine quarrels. They consider this to be a misplaced dissipation of energies and a misuse of opportunities. They wish that every man and woman in India should for the present think of nothing else but political freedom. The first thing is to get rid of the foreigner. Who will rule India and how, what shape will the government of the country take, how will the different religions and different interests be represented therein? — these and other cognate questions do not trouble them. They believe that as soon as England leaves India, some one will rise sphinxlike who will establish some form of national government. The time will produce the man. It would be then time to think and discuss how to improve it. They do not mind if the Hindus or the Mohammedans or the Sikhs or the Gurkhas rule India; nor whether it is the Maharaja of Nepal or that of Odeypore, or that of Baroda, or that of Patiala, or the Nawab of Hyderabad, or that of Bhawalpore, who becomes supreme; nor whether the form of government is monarchical or oligarchic, or republican. These questions do not trouble them. They do not, of course, want any foreign government, but if the way of eventual national freedom lies that way, they do not mind even that. Anything would be better than the present government. The British Government is slowly dissolving the nation. If they have to die, they would rather die of plague or cholera, than of typhoid or consumption. The apprehensions of disturbances of peace do not frighten them. They are sick of peace. Peace under existing conditions has unmanned the nation; it has emasculated the people and sapped their manhood. Anything rather than peace at such price. The desire for peace on any terms, has been the curse of British rule. It has done them more harm than disorder or anarchy ever did. Blessed was the disorder that preceded the rise of the Mahratta power or the establishment of the Sikh commonwealth. Blessed were the conditions of life that produced a Partap, a Sivaji, a Durga Dass, and a Govind Singh.[9] Cursed are the conditions of peace that can only produce Daffadars and Jamadars or at the most Risaldars [10] or Kaiser-Hind-medallists.

This is Hardayalism. Most of the Nationalists of the two classes described above belong to this school, but there are some among them who do not wholly fall in with this view. They are prepared to agree that the political question must always be in the forefront, and that nothing should be done which

[9] Indian heroes.

[10] Non-commissioned officers of the native Indian army.

may in any way overshadow this or relegate it to a secondary position; but they do not believe that politics alone should usurp the whole thought and life of the nation. It would not be right to conclude from the above description that the Indian Nationalists have no *constructive* programme for the future, but it is obvious that in the absence of freedom and opportunities to discuss it openly, opinions on the subject can not be crystallised.

Arabinda Ghosh — Vedantist and Swarajist. It is difficult to say to which of these classes, if to either at all, Arabinda Ghosh belonged or still belongs. At one time it was believed that he belonged to the first class, to which most of the other Bengalee extremists belonged, but whether that belief was right and whether he still thinks on the same lines, it is difficult to say. One thing is certain, that he was and is quite unlike Har Dayal in his line of thought. In intellectual acumen and in scholastic accomplishments he is perhaps superior to Har Dayal, but above all he is deeply religious and spiritual. He is a worshipper of Krishna and is a high-souled Vedantist. Even simpler and more ascetic in his life and habits than Har Dayal, he is for an all-around development of Indian Nationalism. His notions of life and morality are pre-eminently Hindu and he believes in the spiritual mission of his people. His views may better be gathered from an interview, which he recently gave to a correspondent of *The Hindu*, of Madras. We quote the interview almost bodily and in the words of the interviewer.

"But what do you think of the 1914 Congress and Conferences?" I insisted.

He spoke almost with reluctance but in clear and firm accents. He said: "I do not find the proceedings of the Christmas Conferences very interesting and inspiring. They seem to me to be mere repetitions of the petty and lifeless formulas of the past and hardly to show any sense of the great breath of the future that is blowing upon us. I make an exception of the speech of the Congress President which struck me as far above the ordinary level. Some people, apparently, found it visionary and unpractical. It seems to me to be the one practical and vital thing that has been said in India for some time past."

He continued: "The old, petty forms and little narrow, make-believe activities are getting out of date. The world is changing rapidly around us and preparing for more colossal changes in the future. We must rise to the greatness of thought and action which it will demand from the nations who hope to live. No, it is not in any of the old formal activities, but deeper down that I find signs of progress and hope. The last few years have been a period of silence and compression, in which the awakened *Virya*[11] and *Tejas* of the nation have been concentrating for a greater outburst of a better directed energy in the future.

"We are a nation of three hundred millions," added Mr. Ghosh, "inhabiting a great country in which many civilisations have met, full of rich ma-

[11] Force, energy and vitality.

terial and unused capacities. We must cease to think and act like the inhabitants of an obscure and petty village."

"If you don't like our political methods, what would you advise us to do for the realisation of our destiny?"

He quickly replied: "Only by a general intellectual and spiritual awakening can this nation fulfil its destiny. Our limited information, our second-hand intellectual activities, our bounded interests, our narrow life of little family aims and small money getting have prevented us from entering into the broad life of the world. Fortunately, there are ever-increasing signs of a widened outlook, a richer intellectual output and numerous sparks of liberal genius which show that the necessary change is coming. No nation in modern times can grow great by politics alone. A rich and varied life, energetic in all its parts, is the condition of a sound, vigorous national existence. From this point of view also the last five years have been a great benefit to the country."

I then asked what he thought of the vastly improved relations that now exist between the Briton and the Indian in our own country and elsewhere.

"It is a very good thing," he said, and he explained himself in the following manner: "The realisation of our nationhood separate from the rest of humanity was the governing idea of our activities from 1905 to 1910. That movement has served its purpose. It has laid a good foundation for the future. Whatever excesses and errors of speech and action were then disclosed, came because our energy, though admirably inspired, lacked practical experience and knowledge.

"The idea of Indian nationhood is now not only rooted in the public mind, as all recent utterances go to show, but accepted in Europe and acknowledged by the Government and the governing race. The new idea that should now lead us is the realisation of our nationhood not separate from, but in, the future scheme of humanity. When it has realised its own national life and unity, India will still have a part to play in helping to bring about the unity of the nations."

I naturally put in a remark about the Under-Secretary's "Angle of Vision."

"It is well indeed," observed Mr. Ghosh, "that British statesmen should be thinking of India's proper place in the Councils of the Empire, and it is obviously a thought which, if put into effect, must automatically alter the attitude of even the greatest extremists towards the Government and change for the better all existing political relations.

"But it is equally necessary that we, Indians, should begin to think seriously what part Indian thought, Indian intellect, Indian nationhood, Indian spirituality, Indian culture have to fulfil in the general life of humanity. The humanity is bound to grow increasingly on. We must necessarily be in it and of it. Not a spirit of aloofness or of jealous self-defence, but of generous emulation and brotherhood with all men and all nations, justified by a sense of conscious strength, a great destiny, a large place in the human future — this should be the Indian spirit."

The oneness of humanity is a topic dear to the heart of Babu Arabinda Ghosh and when I (*i. e.*, the interviewer) suggested to him that Vedantic ideas would be a good basis for unity, his reply was full of enthusiasm:

"Oh, yes," he said, "I am convinced and have long been convinced that a spiritual awakening, a re-awakening to the true self of a nation is the most important condition of our national greatness. The supreme Indian idea of the oneness of all men in God and its realisation inwardly and outwardly, increasingly even in social relations and the structure of society is destined, I believe, to govern the progress of the human race. India, if it chooses, can guide the world."

And here I said something about our "four thousand" castes, our differences in dress and in "caste marks," our vulgar sectarian antipathies and so on.

"Not so hard, if you please," said Mr. Ghosh with a smile. "I quite agree with you that our social fabric will have to be considerably altered before long. We shall have, of course, to enlarge our family and social life, not in the petty spirit of present day Social Reform, hammering at small details and belittling our immediate past, but with a larger idea and more generous impulses. Our past with all its faults and defects should be sacred to us. But the claims of our future with its immediate possibilities should be still more sacred."

His concluding words were spoken in a very solemn mood:

"It is more important," he said, "that the thought of India should come out of the philosophical school and renew its contact with life, and the spiritual life of India issue out of the cave and the temple and, adapting itself to new forms, lay its hand upon the world. I believe also that humanity is about to enlarge its scope by new knowledge, new powers and capacities, which will create as great a revolution in human life as the physical science of the nineteenth century. Here, too, India holds in her past, a little rusted and put out of use, the key of humanity's future.

"It is in these directions that I have been for some time impelled to turn my energies rather than to the petty political activities which are alone open to us at the present moment. This is the reason of my continued retirement and detachment from action. I believe in the necessity at such times and for such great objects, of *Tapasya,*[12] in silence for self-training, for self-knowledge and storage of spiritual force. Our forefathers used that means, though in different forms. And it is the best means for becoming an efficient worker in the great days of the world."

Ganesh Vináyak Savarkar. At this stage we might mention the name of another Nationalist, who exercised a vast influence on young Indians in England for a number of years and is now serving a life-

[12] Life of meditation and self-denial.

term in the Andamans. We mean Ganesh Vináyak Savarkar. In the simplicity of his life he was of the same class as Arabinda Ghosh and Har Dayal. In the purity of his life he was as high as either. In politics he fell in the first category minus their religious fervour. In his general views he was more or less what Har Dayal is, minus his denunciation of those who are engaged in non-political activities. Savarkar had extremely fine qualities of a leader. He has been caught because he was reckless; he never cared about his personal safety; he had the dash of the old warrior who always put himself in the post of danger. Har Dayal keeps himself in the background and avoids danger. Arabinda stands midway between the two.

The Terrorists. (3) The third class of Nationalists consists of those who would like absolute independence, but who do not believe that it is possible in the near future. They approve of the occasional use of bomb and revolver for terrorist purposes; especially now when no other method has been left of carrying on a propaganda of freedom. The press has been gagged; the platform has been dismantled. Any vigorous political propaganda, including strong criticism of the Government and its methods, is out of the question, No one can point out the political and economic disasters of foreign rule, much less discuss it with reference to actual facts and figures. There is no other way of reminding the people at home and abroad of the standing and colossal wrong which the British Government is guilty of in keeping India under her yoke. In their opinion, the occasional use of the bomb and the revolver is the only way to assert their manhood and their desire for freedom, and to announce their dissatisfaction and discontent. It attracts attention all over the world. It makes people think of India. At home it reminds people of the wrongs they have suffered and are suffering at the hands of the Government. At first it shocks the people, but then it stirs them to think. The bomb has entered Indian life, perhaps never to leave it. They abhor it, but they are getting accustomed to it. They do not now think so badly of those who use the bomb as they once used to.

Advocates of Constructive Nationalisation. (4) In the fourth class are comprised those who want independence, but not *at once.* They would rather consolidate the nation, raise its intellectual and moral tone, increase its economic efficiency, before they raise the standard of revolt. They do not believe that England will ever free them or give them even Colonial Self-Government except under very great pressure. They do not believe that nations let things go out of their grip or hold if they can help it, and unless their own safety demands it. In their opinion the Congress as well as the bomb have come rather early. They would have the nation apply herself wholeheartedly to the work of education and consolidation.

Independence, but not at once. They do not want the British to go until the people of India are sufficiently strong to turn them out by force, and are able to protect themselves and to maintain their independence and their liberties against the outside world. They recognise the force of the argument that the British may never allow them to grow so strong as to be able to win their liberty, and by waiting they might lose all conscious desire for political freedom and might become permanent parasites. They, however, think that they can guard against such possibilities by keeping their nationalism alive and by occasionally suffering for it. Driven to this corner, they admit that now that the Congress and the bomb have come, they might stay. In the opinion of some both are useful in their own way. They would not advocate the use of the bomb and the revolver; in fact they might in all seriousness dissuade people from using them, but when they are used, they would not give up the offenders even if they knew who they were. They would approve the use of the bomb and the revolver against individual tyrants or against people who insult Indian manhood and womanhood, as in the present state of racial and political feeling in India no other way is open to bring them to book and get justice against Englishmen, but they do not like the use of the bomb and the revolver for general political purposes or for terrorising. These people believe in a propaganda of selfless social service. The people must be approached and won over by service and love, before any political upheaval is attempted.

Preparing the Nation for Freedom. Nothing can be achieved without the help of the people. "We must have the people with us," say they. "And in order to win the people to our side, we must show them conclusively that we have their interests at heart, that we love them perhaps more than we love ourselves, that we are disinterested and public spirited and that we are in every respect better and more honourable than the foreign rulers. Our moral superiority over the agents of the foreign government must be ever present in the minds of the people in order to enable them to support us and back us in the coming political struggle." In their eyes the Congress propaganda has no other value but educational. They have no faith in the benevolence of British statesmen and they do not believe that the Congress would achieve anything substantial. They are very uncertain about the future, and therefore to them, the best course open is to engage in educational and social work. They are neither dreamers nor idealists, but practical patriots, who are content to do the spade work and sow the seed. They confess that they can not see far ahead and are therefore afraid of the demoralising influences of the bomb and the revolver. Nor can they justify political robberies and dacoities. They think that, this time, independence should come never to be lost again, and in their judgment that is only possible if independence is not won by a few but by the whole united nation. In the meantime they would wait and build up their nation.

Preparatory Work from Below. The Congress has failed, they say, because it has been trying to get political concessions from above. The right policy is to work from below. They do not believe in "mendicancy"; nor do they place any reliance in "benevolence and philanthropy in politics." On the other hand, they differ from the extremists in their methods, as they believe in a steady development of the national mind and the national will and have no faith in heroic remedies. They do not care to run the risk of "relapses." They contain in their number some of the noblest sons of India, whose life is a record of continuous selfless service in the field of social work. They should not be confounded with the "resolution" patriots of the Social Conferences or other conferences; nor should they be judged by the length of their speeches or their fluency or capacity to deliver long orations in English. They are generally modest people who do not claim erudite scholarship or great statesmanship. They do not go in for any recognition, whether from the Government or from the people. The satisfaction of their own conscience and undisturbed work are the only rewards they seek.

Brahmo Samaj, Arya Samaj, Ramakrishna Mission. They are to be found in all sections of the great Indian nation, in all religions, and in all communities. They live simply on simple fare, in simple and scanty garments and in simple houses. They earn in order to give. They live in order to serve. To this class belong *some* of the Bengalee deportees, and to this class belong a great many members of the Brahmo Samaj, the Arya Samaj, and the Ramakrishna Mission. They have large followings, but yet their number is by no means great. They are well known in their respective circles, but are not so well known outside, as the "extremists" and "moderates" are. The C. I. D. (Criminal Investigation Department) of the Government keeps a close watch over them; the government officers keep themselves informed of their movements and doings. They want to be left alone and allowed to do their work quietly and unostentatiously, but the Government will not leave them alone and suspects them of deep designs and secret propaganda.

The Moderates. (5) We now come to the moderates. There are some who would not advocate the use of the bomb or the revolver, but who do not desire the total disappearance of the extremist party; and the occasional use of the bomb and the revolver gives a point to their organisation which they would not lose. Lacking the intelligent support of the masses in their propaganda, being too lazy to court it by legitimate means, or too self-centred to run the risk involved therein, they are heartily glad of the existence of a party in the country which has raised their importance in the eyes of the Government and the British public. Of course they do not say so and their abhorrence and detestation of the bomb and the revolver is quite genuine, yet they would be very sorry if the extremist party were extirpated altogether.

Gokhale. The noblest and the best of the Congress type from the Nationalist point of view was represented by Mr. Gokhale. Mr. Gokhale loved his country quite sincerely and lived and worked for it. With the exception of Dadabhai Naoroji, he was the only Congressman of reputation and name that

G. K. GOKHALE

lived for his country only and gave his all to her service. His life was fairly simple; his patriotism was of the highest type; yet he was not the type of man fitted to be a hero. He had the qualities of statesmanship, but lacked those of generalship. He objected to people designating his policy as one of mendicancy, or questioning his political ideals. He used to remonstrate and say in the most touching way: "Do you think, my friend, we are so devoid of self-respect and so base as to be happy at our country being under foreign domination; do you think we wish that it should always remain under foreign yoke? No, you do us great injustice if you think so. I would have my country be free to-day if that were possible. But is it possible? Can we work on that basis? In politics you must consider what is practical and what is unpractical. We can in no way bind the future generations. Who are we to bind them irrevocably? We are doing what we in our own times consider best and practicable. We are not beggars and our policy is not that of mendicancy. We are ambassadors of our people at a foreign court, to watch and guard the interests of our country and get as much for her as we can. That is our position." Mr. Gokhale believed in the work of consolidation and in the work for increasing the social efficiency of the people of India regardless of caste, creed, or colour. He had a great deal in common with class number (4). But he had great faith in political agitation on moderate lines. He was fully conscious of the weakness of the Congress methods and extremely disliked the behaviour of some of the leaders. He quite bemoaned their lack of enthusiasm, their want of self-sacrifice, their intolerance, the lack of spirit of true comradeship in them, their self-sufficiency and, last but not least, their luxurious lives. He often compared the type of human material which found its way into the Congress with those who joined the ranks of the extremists. He admired the spirit of the latter, their devotion to the cause, their asceticism and their selflessness. He wished he had some of that stuff to work for the Congress. He admired Arabinda and Har Dayal. He used to say that he could not see very far ahead and therefore he preferred to work for the immediate future. A few days before his departure from England he said to two of his most intimate friends (husband and wife) that India would be free in 25 years. What he meant by freedom we do not know. Probably he meant "as free as the self-governed colonies." Of late he was losing faith in English liberalism. He noticed the lack of great minds among the liberals, but he said they were the only people with whom we could work. His experiences on the Royal Commission for Public Services saddened the last days of his life. He could not bear the insults that witness after witness (from among the Anglo-Indians) heaped on his countrymen, their character, their honesty, and their capacity. He objected to the extremists calling themselves nationalists to the exclusion of the people of his ways of thinking. He said we were all nationalists. He was by far the noblest of the moderates. There is no one who is even half so good and noble as he was.

Congress Leaders. A great many Congress leaders are true patriots, but they have such an abnormal love of peace and luxury, that they can not even think of methods which might even remotely result in disturbances of peace, in riots, and in disasters. Hence their detestation of the extremist methods and their distrust of carrying on a propaganda among the masses. They would proceed very, very slowly. Of course, there are some among them who are cowards, some who are self-seekers, who hanker after judgeships, memberships, knighthoods, and so on, but we do not count them as nationalists, and history knows of no political party which was absolutely free from such weaknesses. There are some among the Congressmen who are moderates by profession, but extremists in their ways of thinking, lacking the courage of identifying themselves with the latter; just as there are some who are Congressmen in name, but are really out and out loyalists seeking opportunities of advancing their own interests. Then there are some who favour constitutional agitation, but want to make the Congress more self-assertive and self-sufficient. They would pass resolutions on current topics but would have no petitioning or praying or memorialising.

Passive Resisters. There are others who would go even farther and inaugurate a campaign of passive resistance and boycott. The Congress thus claims as many types of nationalists as the extremists. The Passive Resisters are likely to come to the front if Mr. Gandhi, the great Hindu Passive Resister, undertakes to organise them.

For obvious reasons we can not classify the living Indian Nationalists in India by name.

CHAPTER VI

INDIAN NATIONALISM AND THE WORLD-FORCES

Inspiration through European Nationalism. There can be no doubt that Indian nationalism is receiving a great deal of support from the world-forces operating outside of India. On the political side it has been inspired and strengthened by the forces of European nationalism — the struggles and successes of the English proletariat, the sufferings and the eventual triumph of the French revolutionists, the efforts and victories of the Italians, the continued struggle of Russians, Poles, Finns, Hungarians, and others. The Indian nationalist is an ardent student of the history of Modern Europe, of England, France, Germany, Netherlands, Italy, Russia, Austria, and last but not least, of Turkey and the Balkan States. The Nationalist Calendar of great men followed by young India contains such names as those of Washington, Cavour, Mazzini, Bismarck, Kossuth, Emmet, Parnell, by the side of Partap, Ram Das, Guru Govind Singh, Sivajī, Tipú Sultan, and the Ranī of Jhansī.

History of Modern Europe tabooed in Universities. The Indian Government is conscious of this, and some people think this is what is influencing the policy of the Indian universities in tabooing the history of Modern Europe from the courses of studies.

American literature and American events are also playing their own part in the influences that are feeding Indian nationalism. The leaders are and have ever been close students of American literature and the history of the American Federation. Asia, however, is playing a greater part in moulding and influencing Indian nationalism. The Russo-Japanese War thrilled India to its core. The recognition of Japan as a great power by the Concert of Europe is regarded by Young India as the potent factor in Indian Nationalism. An awakening current passed through the country electrifying the most inert, inarticulate and otherwise unapproachable sections of the populations. Then came the events in Turkey, in Russia, and in China.

Italian-Turko War. Turkey's war with Italy, followed by her struggle with the Balkan States, has done wonders in nationalising the Indian Mohammedans. At the present moment the Mohammedans perhaps feel even more intensely than the Hindus.

Indian patriots travelling abroad study the current problems of the various countries through which they pass, and note their bearing on their own national problems. But what is most important is, that they seek and get opportunities of meeting and conversing with the nationalists of other countries. Some of them are in close touch with the Egyptian and Irish nationalists, others with Persians, and so on. Indian nationalism is thus entering on an international phase which is bound to strengthen it and bring it into the arena of world forces.

Interpretation of India to Western World. Indian thought, Indian history, and Indian culture are receiving a great deal more attention now than they ever did before. There is hardly an important contribution to the thought of the world which does not notice and consider the Indian view of the matter under discussion. But India is seen by the world only through Western spectacles. Some Indians are doing valuable work in interpreting India to the Western world, and their work is attracting notice; but a great deal yet remains to be done and Indian scholars should make it an item of their programme to open India and Indian thought to the outsiders and thus bring India into the vortex of world forces.

Tagorism. While Rabindra Nath Tagore is to some degree losing in the estimation and affection of his own countrymen by somewhat sacrificing nationalism to art, he is gaining in world reputation. Tagorism is becoming a cult and he is at the present moment perhaps the most popular and most widely read and widely admired literary man in the world. It was a mere chance that his work attracted the notice of the trustees of the Nobel prize trust. He himself did nothing to attract their notice.

The Indian publicist has so far lived in a world of his own. He has ignored or paid very scanty attention to the forces operating in the world for progress, for liberty, and for advance in democratic ways. The leaders of the National Congress have never tried to enlist sympathy for their cause anywhere outside England. They have never realised the value of the world forces and the great sensitiveness of the English as to what the world thinks and says of them.

The Indian Nationalist would do well to note this. He should begin to think and act internationally. It is impossible to separate India altogether from the rest of the world, however the British might try and whatever they might do. For her sons to try to do that is to strengthen their chains and add to the weight which is crushing their country. Nothing could be more suicidal or more short-sighted.

CHAPTER VII

THE RELIGIOUS AND THE COMMUNAL ELEMENTS IN INDIAN NATIONALISM

FOR a time the Mohammedan minority was the hope of the British Government in India. As far back as 1888, Lord Dufferin[1] and Sir Auckland Colvin had successfully appealed to their fears, and won them over by promises of preferential treatment. That policy has been consistently followed since then, and so far has been a great success. The bulk of the educated Mohammedans has opposed the Congress, in order to please the Government and win their gratitude; they also opposed the *Swadeshi* Movement, although the success of the *Swadeshi* was likely to benefit them very materially, since the handloom industry was principally in their hands. In return, they received substantial benefits in the shape of large grants of money for educational purposes, a larger percentage of posts in government service, a larger number of titles and honours, a separate and larger representation in the councils, and so on. Lord Morley confirmed this policy of preference by making it a special feature of his Re-

[1] Lord Dufferin was the Governor General of India and Sir A. Colvin was the Lieutenant Governor of what were then the Northwestern Provinces, now the United Provinces of Agra and Oudh.

form scheme in 1908. So the Mohammedans were in very high spirits in 1908. The Nationalist party in Bengal had a large number of friends and sympathisers among the Mohammedans, but as compared with the Separatist party, their number was very small and meagre. In its inception and for some time thereafter the Nationalist movement in India was thus a pre-eminently Hindu movement.

Mohammedan Revulsion of Feeling against the British. The world events of the last four years, however, have changed the whole aspect of affairs in India. The events in Turkey, in Tripoli, in Egypt and in Persia have affected the Mohammedans deeply and have brought about a revulsion of feeling against the British. The Muslims are a virile and proud people. The attitude of Britain towards Turkey has offended their deepest susceptibilities and they have begun to think that the British in India wanted to bribe them into silent acquiescence in what was happening to the Muslim people in the other parts of the globe. For the last four years the Muslim press has been carrying on a strong, vigorous pan-Islamic propaganda. The Mohammedan classes as well as masses are full of veiled and subdued hatred of the British. Sometimes this finds expression on the platform, in the press, and in permanent literature also. In the last Balkan war and during Turkey's conflict with Italy about Tripoli, the Mohammedan mosques rang with loud prayers for the victory of Turkey, and with strong and open denunciation of their Christian enemies. There is a perceptible and clear change in the political pronouncements of the Muslim League,[2] but the political influence of the Muslim League among the people was, so far, little as compared with the influence of the Pan-Islamic party. This Pan-Islamic party is the extreme wing of the Mohammedan Nationalists.

The number of forfeitures of the Moslem papers and publications under the Press Act, the nature of those publications and the continued support given to the papers that have been more than once forfeited and punished by the Government, the change in the tone of the Moslem papers in their comments on government measures, and the newly born *entente* between the Hindus and Mohammedans, of which there is unmistakable proof in the press as well as in actual life, all point in the same direction. There is every chance of the Hindu extremists and Muslim extremists making an alliance and joining hands, while even the Mohammedan moderates are coming nearer the Hindu moderates.[3] The former may not actually join the Congress in large numbers, but they are thinking and acting the same way. The Mohammedan moderates are wiser than the Hindu moderates. They use their extreme party as a trump card in their negotiations with the Government more effectively than the Hindus do or have ever done. The Mohammedan extremist receives more substantial support and sympathy from his moderate co-religionist than the Hindu extremist does from the Hindu moderates. The Moham-

[2] The organisation of the Pro-British Muslims.
[3] See the Introduction.

medan moderate is more outspoken in his criticism of government measures that injuriously affect the Mohammedans; he is less lavish in his praises of the British Raj; he is a more skilful negotiator and a decidedly better and more successful diplomat.

The educated Mohammedans, outside India, are almost to a man identified with Indian Nationalism. So the Indian Mohammedan's changed sentiments towards the British are likely to be a source of great strength to the national cause and make the situation more hopeful from the point of view of Indian Nationalism.

Disaffection among the Sikhs. But the Mohammedans were not the only people whom the Britishers had succeeded in keeping aloof from the Hindu Nationalists. The Sikhs had also so far kept aloof. The treatment of the Sikhs in Canada, the *Komagata Maru*[4] incident and the influence of Har Dayal and the Gadar party on the Pacific Coast of America formed by him, have affected a great change of feeling among the Sikhs also. The Government may try to win them back by making concessions and conferring preferments, but a move like the one recently made in giving Mr. K. G. Gupta's seat on the Secretary of State's Council in London to Sirdar Daljit Singh, a Sikh nobleman, is likely to make them look even more ridiculous than before. The

[4] *Komagata Maru* is the name of a Japanese steamer, which a number of Sikh emigrants chartered in Hong Kong in 1914 A. D. in order to take them to Canada. They were not allowed to land and were forced to return to India, under circumstances which have created a bitter anti-British feeling among the Indians all over the world.

Britisher's lack of imagination is colossal, but we did not know that the war was likely to affect even his sense of humour.

CHAPTER VIII

THE FUTURE

It is both difficult and risky to predict, especially concerning a country situated as India is to-day. It is always the unexpected that happens in human affairs. This is particularly true where human affairs are so complicated and complex as in India. It is perhaps easier to predict the future of America or England, than that of India. The Indian nationalists of the nineties, or even of the early days of the new century, could hardly have imagined the developments of the last fifteen years. It is true that India is rather immobile; its masses are rather inert; and perhaps of all peoples the least affected by changes in the outside world. They have been under the benumbing influence of a philosophy of life which keeps them contented even under adverse circumstances, even when they are starving and have no clothes to hide their nakedness.

Change in Indian Life and Depth of Nationalism. But this is only partially true of modern India. There is a great deal of exaggeration about the immobility of Indian people. There may be millions in India who are as unaffected by modern conditions of life and modern ideas as they were fifty years ago, but then there are millions who have consciously awakened. Their strength is not to be judged by the attendance at Congresses and conferences or other public meetings or demonstrations, nor by the circulation of newspapers or books. Popular demonstrations organised in honour of popular leaders, and the increase in the circulation of newspapers give indications of a great change in Indian life, but the actual change is even much greater. Read the poetry of the country or its prose, read the rough versifyings of the half-educated or even uneducated men and women (including some who are even illiterate), listen to the talk in the village park or square or other meeting places, see the games which the children of rustics and the poorest classes play, attend to the patterings of children, examine the popular songs or the music that is now in demand, then you will see how deeply nationalism has pervaded Indian life and what a strong hold it has gained in the thoughts of the people. No foreigner can realise that; only an Indian can properly understand it. Examine the vernacular press — the most sober and the most loyal papers, and underlying the expressions of deepest loyalty, you would assuredly come across genuine tears of blood, shed for the misfortune of the country, its decline, its present wretched and miserable condition. From the Indian press we hear a never-ceasing lamentation. Listen to the utterances of the most wanton chief, and the most callous millionaire, bring him out from his isolation or retirement, put him on the public platform, and you will notice a vein of nationalism in his thoughts and in his words. But if you can know what he talks in private to friends from whom he keeps no secrets, you will see and notice a great deal more. The writer has not so far met a single Indian of any class — he has met Indians of all classes and of all shades of opinions, educated, uneducated, prince and peasant, moderate and extremist, loyalist and seditionist,— who was genuinely sorry at the outbreak of this war. A number of Indians are fighting at the front. They are sincerely loyal and true to their oath of allegiance. They would leave nothing undone to win, but in their heart of hearts lurks something which in moments of reflection or when they are off duty, reminds them of the wrongs which they and their countrymen are suffering at the hands of England. Nationalism is no longer confined to the classes. It promises to become a universal cult. It is permeating the masses. Only those Indians realise it who mix with the people and do not derive their knowledge from works written by Englishmen or by other arm-chair politicians. No foreigner, however kind and sympathetic, however great his knowledge of the language of the country, can ever realise it fully. Even the dancing girls are affected by it. They will sing political or national songs if you so wish. Even the wandering minstrel with his rude, one-stringed instrument, knows the song that is likely to bring him help.

Nationalism Fertilised by Blood of Martyrs. No amount of repression or espionage can stop it. No amount of official terrorism and no devices, invented or followed to inculcate loyalty, can stop or check the flow of the new feeling of patriotism and nationalism which is being constantly fed by the sentences of death and transportation that the British courts are passing on beardless youths. The Government can not help it. They must punish the offender and the criminal. They must hunt up the seditionist. They would not be a government if they would do otherwise, but India is now in that stage and Indian nationalism is in that condition when repression, death sentences, and imprisonments are more beneficial to it than otherwise. The more it is repressed and suppressed, the more this spirit grows and spreads. It is a seed that is richly fertilised by the blood of martyrs. The people do not argue, they do not reason, they do not analyse; they feel that good, well-connected, healthy, beautiful boys are dying in the country's cause and to get a redress of the country's wrongs. When a bomb is thrown, the people genuinely condemn the bomb thrower, are sincere in their detestation, but when he is hanged or transported, they are sorry for him. Their original abhorrence changes into sympathy and then into love. They are martyrs of the national cause. They may be misguided, even mad, but they are martyrs all the same. The moralist and the legalist and the loyalist and the constitutionalist, all condemn their deeds, but the doers themselves, they adore, and their names they enshrine in their hearts.

Wave of Indian Nationalism is on. Such is human psychology, and such is the psychology of nations in the making. The Indian mind has entered on that phase. No amount of sweet speeches by the Viceroy or by the Lieutenant Governors or by the commissioners or deputy commissioners, no amount of honours and titles or rewards to individuals, no amount of preferment of one community as against another, no amount of canal-making or railway-developing, can change the tide that has begun to flow, or retard the sweep, much less turn it to ebb.

Propitiation and Petty Concessions Futile. This is the supreme fact of Indian life which every one who has anything to do with India, official or non-official, statesman or layman, politician or publicist, must recognise and face. Nations and individuals, filled with their own importance, drunk with power and resources, accustomed to mould things and forces in their own way, determined to keep what they have got, may not see things which are unpleasant to look at or to think about. But facts are facts and do not wait for their action on the pleasure of those who do not like them. Canute-like they may command the waves, but the waves will not listen to them. The wave of Indian nationalism is on and no amount of tinkering with Indian administration, or sweet phrases, or promises can check it. "We are the subjects of the same sovereign," "citizens of the same empire," "brothers in arms," "comrades," and so on,—these are kind words spoken by people who perhaps mean well. But in the light of past experience they do not carry much weight; they may befool some soft-hearted people, but they would not affect the general mind of the nation so long as they remain unaccompanied by deeds. An Executive Council for the United Provinces, a High Court for the Punjab, a High Court and a University for Behar, a Charter to the Hindu University, liberal grants to Islamic schools and colleges, may please some barristers and pleaders, but they will not satisfy the nation, so long as the Arms Act is on the statute book, so long as the Indian Councils are a farce, so long as the fiscal policy is laid down in the interests of Lancashire, and so long as hundreds and thousands of Indian boys fail to earn a decent living, while the country is being ruled and exploited by the few fortunate foreigners. Indians want to go to Canada, to South Africa, to the United States of America, because the wages to be earned in India are so low, because the life at home is so miserable, so helpless and so hard and so humiliating. Even abroad the Indian is kicked and insulted at almost every step, but then that is more easily borne than the kicks and insults of Englishmen in India.

Internal Division no Valid Plea. India has and can produce enough to feed her own children,[1] nay to spare, provided she were free to make her own laws, spend her own revenues, and protect her industries. Those who plead that Indians are too hopelessly divided into religions, communities, sects, castes, and languages, to be able to form a government of their own, forget that the English have been in India only for the last century and a half and that

[1] During her most dreadful famines hundreds of thousands of tons of foodstuffs were shipped out of India.

before that India governed herself. The India of to-day is in no way happier than it was before pre-British days. The India of Akbar was happier than the England of Elizabeth and even more prosperous. The India of Asoka was infinitely happier and more prosperous than the England of Alfred the Great. The India of Aurangzeb may perhaps have been miserable, but surely not more miserable than the England of Henry VIII, or the England of James I, or the Scotland of Mary, or the Ireland of Cromwell, or the France of Henry IV, or the Holland of Philip. We have the testimony of English historians and observers that subjects of the East India Company were in no way happier or more prosperous than when they were under Native rule,[2] and the subjects of Native States in India governed by Natives are on the whole in no way worse off than British subjects under the direct rule of the British.

Look at the United States, how the varied races, sects, religions, and communities have merged their differences and live under one national government; look at the number of languages spoken in the United States — in their schools and in their factories. Look at Switzerland, what a tiny little country it is! How many languages are spoken and taught in its schools and how many languages are spoken and used in its councils, and how many religions are professed by the people of the country!

[2] See Mill's History of British India, Vol. VI, pp. 149, 150, Vol. VII, p. 388, and p. 393, Vol. IX, pp. 207, 209. See Bishop Heber's description of India in 1824 quoted in Mill and Wilson's History of India, Vol. IX, p. 376. Also that of Mr. Shore in 1833.

The same remarks may be made about the dual monarchy of Austria-Hungary, where the form of government is largely representative in spite of the diversity of races, sects and languages.

The number of religions, sects and languages in India has been grossly exaggerated. With every census the number goes up by hundreds, though the country and the people are the same.

Illiteracy the Fault of the British and no Bar to Self-government. Again it is sometimes said that India cannot be self-ruling because of its illiteracy. This argument does not come with good grace from the Britishers because it is they who are responsible for the appalling illiteracy of the Indian population. In Japan, where the work of education was begun late in the last century, 28 per cent. of the children of school age were at school in 1873; by 1902–1903 the percentage had risen to 90. In India, after 150 years of British rule, the percentage is 19.6. The Indian Nationalists have for a number of years been asking for compulsory universal education, but the Government would not listen. The late Mr. Gokhale's Compulsory Elementary Education Bill was strongly opposed by the Government and thrown out. But what is even worse is that the Government would not let the people open their own schools and colleges because of the unreasonably high standard set up by the Department for their recognition as public schools.

However, universal literacy of the people is not an indispensable pre-requisite of self-rule. In Japan, where 50 years ago representative government was set up, only the *Samurai* were literate. In India, too, the higher classes are educated to a considerable extent.

England has enjoyed parliamentary government for centuries, but universal education was only introduced in 1870.

Internal Troubles. As for internal troubles following the withdrawal of the British or the grant of self-government we ask, "Is there any country on the face of the earth which is free from internal troubles?" Even Great Britain is not; much less are the self-governing colonies. Yet nobody questions their right to govern themselves. Only the other day President Wilson considered the existence of internal disorder in Mexico to be no justification for the United States interfering in its affairs.

Unfitness of Orientals for Representative Institutions. As for the unfitness of Orientals for democratic institutions, why the ancient history of India refutes it almost conclusively. India was the home of democratic institutions long before England and France had any notion of what democracy implied. But if any further proof of the absurdity of this plea was needed that has been furnished by Japan.

Nationalism has come to Stay. Let England try an experiment by repealing the Arms Act and giving a parliamentary government to India and see if these considerations effectively stand in the way of progress. Be that as it may, however, one thing seems to be assured and certain, that Indian nationalism can neither be killed nor suppressed by repression, nor by minor concessions. Nationalism has come to stay and will stay. What will be the upshot is only known to the Gods. England may win or lose in the great war in which she is engaged. Indian nationalism will gain in either case. We need not consider how India will fare if England loses. She may come under Mohammedan domination, or the Germans may take possession of her; the English would be gone and then India would enter upon a new life. India does not want it. She will resist it with all her strength. But if it comes she can't help it and Great Britain would be responsible for having brought it. In case, however, England wins, as she is likely to, the Indian nationalism will still gain. There will be a demand for political advance, for a change in the political status of the country and in its relations towards England and her colonies. From what we know of English temper, of English political machinery, of English political methods, of English ways and of English history, that demand is sure to be refused. Some minor, petty concessions may be made, but they would be disproportionate to the sacrifices of men and money that India is making in the war. They will not satisfy the country. Disaffection and discontent will grow and that is the kind of food on which nationalism thrives and prospers. So long as there are Curzons, Macdonnels, and Sydenhams in the English Parliament, Indian nationalism will not starve for want of congenial food. And we have no reason to think that these dignitaries of the British Government are likely to disappear.

Curzons, Macdonnels, Sydenhams, responsible for Bombs and Revolvers. These persons are directly responsible for the appearance of bombs and revolvers in Indian political life. The young men who use them are mere tools of circumstances. If any persons deserve to be hanged for the use of these destructive machines by Indian nationalists, it is they. It is a pity that while the latter are dying by tens on the scaffold, the former should be free to carry on their propaganda of racial discrimination, racial hatred, and social preferment. But the ways of Providence are inscrutable. It is perhaps some higher dispensation that is using these miserable Junkers for its own purposes. Indians have faith in Providence and they believe that what is happening is for the best. The Indians are a chivalrous people; they will not disturb England as long as she is engaged with Germany. The struggle after the war might, however, be even more bitter and more sustained.

A SHORT BIBLIOGRAPHY OF BOOKS IN ENGLISH

Books by Englishmen

"New Spirit in India" by H. W. Nevinson.
"The Awakening in India" by J. Ramsay MacDonald, M.P.
"India, Impressions and Suggestions" by J. Keir Hardie, M.P.
"New India" by Sir Henry Cotton (once an M.P.), late of the Indian Civil Service.
"Allen Octavian Hume" by Sir W. Wedderburn, late of the Indian Civil Service (once an M.P.).
"Prosperous British India" by Mr. William Digby, C.I.E.
"India and the Empire" by Mrs. Annie Besant.
"Indian Nationalism" by Edwyn Bevan.
"Bureaucratic Government" by Bernard Houghton (late of the Indian Civil Service).
"Lord Curzon a Failure." by C. J. O'Donnell (late of the Indian Civil Service).
"Causes of Indian Discontent" by C. J. O'Donnell (late of the Indian Civil Service).
"The Indian Ryot" by Sir W. Wedderburn.
"The Skeleton at the Jubilee Feast" by Sir W. Wedderburn.
"Congress Green Books" (84, 85, Palace Chambers, Westminster, London).

"The New Nationalist Movement in India," by Dr. J. T. Sunderland.
"Indian Famines and Their Cause" by Dr. J. T. Sunderland, 423 West 120th Street, New York.

Books by Indians

"Poverty or Un-British Rule in India" by Dadabhai Naoroji.
"India Under Early British Rule" by R. C. Dutt, C.I.E.
"India in the Victorian Age" by R. C. Dutt, C.I.E.
"Famines and Land Assessment" by R. C. Dutt, C.I.E.
"England and India" (Indian Progress, 1785-1885) by R. C. Dutt, C.I.E.
"The Civilization of India" by R. C. Dutt, C.I.E.
"Speeches of the Honourable Mr. G. K. Gokhale."
"The Swadeshi, a Symposium."
"Recent Indian Finance" by Wacha.
"The National Evolution" by A. C. Mazumdar.
"The Indian National Congress."
"Speeches of Sir P. M. Mehta."
"The Story of My Deportation" by Lajpat Rai.
"The Alipore [Bomb Case] Trial."

Periodicals

The Modern Review (monthly). Calcutta.
The Indian Review (monthly). Madras.
The Hindustan Review (monthly). Allahabad.
India (the British Organ of the Indian National Congress, weekly). London.

APPENDICES

I

EXTRACTS FROM SIR HENRY COTTON'S "NEW INDIA."

Feudatory Chiefs Powerless. "It would perhaps be ungenerous to probe too narrowly the dependent position and consequent involuntary action of the feudatory chiefs. They are powerless to protect themselves. There is no judicial authority to which they can appeal. There is no public opinion to watch their interests. Technically independent under the suzerainty of the Empire, they are practically held in complete subjection. Their rank and honours depend on the pleasure of a British Resident at their Court, and on the secret and irresponsible mandates of a Foreign Office at Simla" (page 34).

Gross Insults to Indians. "That intense Anglo-Saxon spirit of self-approbation which is unpleasantly perceptible in England itself, and is so often offensive among vulgar Englishmen on the Continent, very soon becomes rampant in India.

"There are innumerable instances in which pedestrians have been abused and struck because they have not lowered their umbrellas at the sight of a sahib on the highway. There are few Indian gentlemen even of the highest rank who have not had experience of gross insults when travelling by railway, because Englishmen object to sit in the same carriage with a native" (pages 68–69).

II

SOME OPINIONS ABOUT BRITISH INDIA

Industrial Ruin of India. Gokhale. "When we come to this question of India's Industrial domination by England, we come to what may be described as the most deplorable result of British rule in this country. In other matters there are things on the credit side and things on the debit side. . . . But when you come to the industrial field, you will find that the results have been disastrous. You find very little here on the credit side and nearly all the entries on the debit side. Now this is a serious statement to make, but I think it can be substantiated."

India a Mere Possession. Gokhale. "India formed the largest part of the Empire, but was governed as a mere possession of the British people. Three features showed that it had no part or lot in the Empire. In the first place, the people were kept disarmed; it was thought to be dangerous to allow them to carry arms. Secondly, they had absolutely no voice in the government of their own country; they were expressly disqualified from holding certain high offices, and practically excluded from others. Lastly, they were not allowed a share in the privileges of the Empire in any portion outside British India, except a limited one in the United Kingdom itself."—MR. GOKHALE.

Masses Starved. Sir C. A. Elliott. "I do not hesitate to say that half our agricultural population never know from year's end to year's end what it is to have their hunger fully satisfied."—SIR C. A. ELLIOTT, one-time Lieut.-Governor of Bengal.

Sir W. W. Hunter. In 1880. "There remain forty millions of people who go through life on insufficient food."—SIR W. W. HUNTER.

William Digby. In 1893. The *Pioneer* sums up Mr. Grierson's facts regarding the various sections of the population in Gaya: "Briefly, it is that all the persons of the labouring classes, and ten per cent. of the cultivating and artisan classes, or forty-five per cent. of the total population, are insufficiently clothed, or insufficiently fed, or both. In Gaya district this would give about a million persons without sufficient means of support. If we assume that the circumstances of Gaya are not exceptional,—and there is no reason for thinking otherwise—it follows that nearly one hundred millions of people in British India are living in extreme poverty."

In 1901. "The poverty and suffering of the people are such as to defy description. In fact, for nearly fifteen years there has been *a continuous famine in India* owing to high prices."

70,000,000 *Continually Hungry People in British India. W. Digby.* "Since Sir William Hunter's remarks were made the population has increased (or is alleged to have increased) by nearly thirty millions. Meanwhile the income of the Empire has greatly decreased during this period. Wherefore this follows: that is, if with the same income, in 1880 forty millions were insufficiently fed, the additional millions cannot have had, cannot now have, enough to eat; this, again, ensues:—

40,000,000 plus, say, 30,000,000, make 70,000,000; and *there are this number of continually hungry people in British India at the beginning of the Twentieth Century.*" —William Digby, C. I. E.

Deaths from Famine or Consequent Diseases, 1891 *to* 1900 *alone:* estimated by a correspondent of the *Lancet,* 19,000,000.

Total area under cultivation. In the year 1911–12, the *total area* under *food grains* was over 195 *million acres,* plus 7.5, *i. e.* over 202½ *million acres.*

In 1912–13, India *exported foodstuffs* of the value of over 260 million dollars.

In 1913–14 she exported about 216 million dollars' worth of foodstuffs.

Famines of Money, not Food. Lord G. Hamilton. "The recent famines are famines of money, and not of food."—LORD G. HAMILTON, former Secretary of State.

Causes of Famines. 1. National industries deliberately crushed by the East India Co. cannot revive under existing conditions.

2. Annual drain of India.

3. Lack of such education as will enable people to develop their resources.

Drain. Montgomery Martin. "The annual drain of £3,000,000 from British India has mounted in thirty years, at 12 per cent. (the usual Indian rate) compound interest, to the enormous sum of £723,900,000 sterling."—MONTGOMERY MARTIN. (In 1830.)

Digby. "During the last thirty years of the century the average drain cannot have been far short of £30,000,000 per year, or, in the thirty years, £900,000,000, not reckoning interest!"—SIR WILLIAM DIGBY.

Enormous Foreign Tribute. Rev. J. T. Sunderland. Rev. J. T. Sunderland in his work "The Causes of Famine in India," like all impartial writers, has conclusively proved that neither "failure of rains" nor "over population" is the cause of famines in India. He has stated that the real cause of famine is the extreme, the abject, the awful poverty of the Indian people caused by "*Enormous Foreign Tribute,*" "British Indian Imperialism" and the destruction of Indian industries.

Government assessment too high. Sir W. Hunter. "The government assessment does not leave enough food to the cultivator to support himself and his family throughout the year."—SIR WILLIAM HUNTER, K. C. S. I., in the Viceroy's Council, 1883.

The Ryot. Herbert Compton. "There is no more pathetic figure in the British Empire than the Indian peasant. His masters have ever been unjust to him. He is ground until everything has been expressed, except the marrow of his bones."—MR. HERBERT COMPTON in "Indian Life," 1904.

Hindustan is an extensive agricultural country and the average land produces two crops a year, and in Bengal there are lands which produce thrice a year. Bengal alone produces such large crops that they are quite sufficient to provide *all the population of Hindustan for two years.*

Indian Plunder. Adam Brooks. Adam Brooks says, ("Laws of Civilization and Decay," page 259–246) "Very soon after the Battle of Plassey (fought in 1757) the Bengal Plunder began to arrive in London and the effect appears to have been almost instantaneous. Probably since the world began, no investment has yielded the profit reaped from the Indian plunder. The amount of treasure wrung from the conquered people and transferred from India to English banks between Plassey and Waterloo (57 years) has been variously estimated at from $2,500,000,000 to $5,000,000,000. The methods of plunder and embezzlement, by which every Briton in India enriched himself during the earlier history of the East India Company, gradually passed away, but the drain did not pass away. The difference between that earlier day and the present is, that India's tribute to England is obtained by "indirect methods," under forms of law. It is estimated by Mr. Hyndman that at least $175,000,000 is drained away every year from India, without a cent's return."

Swami Abhedananda. "India pays interest on England's debt, which in 1900 amounted to 244 millions sterling, and which annually increases. Besides this, she pays for all the officers, civil and military, and a huge standing army, pensions of officers, and even the cost of the India Building in London, as well as the salary of every menial servant of that house. For 1901–2 the total expenditure charged against revenue was $356,971,410.00, out of which $84,795,515.00 was spent in England as Home Charges, not including the pay of European officers in India, saved and remitted to England.—SWAMI ABHEDANANDA ("India and Her People").

Alfred Webb (late M.P.): "In charges for the India

Office (in London); for recruiting (in Great Britain, for soldiers to serve in India); for civil and military pensions (to men now living in England, who were formerly in the Indian service); for pay and allowances on furloughs (to men on visits to England); for private remittances and consignments (for India to England); for interest on Indian debt (paid to parties in England); and for interest on railways and other works (paid to shareholders in England), there is annually drawn from India and spent in the United Kingdom, a sum calculated at from £25,000,000 to £30,000,000 (Between $125,000,000 and $150,000,000)."

"*Narrow and Shortsighted Imperial Policy.*" *Sir Archibald R. Colquehoun.* "The present condition of affairs undoubtedly renders the struggle for existence a hard one, as may be realized when it is considered that a vast population of India not only from the inevitable droughts which so frequently occur, *but also from a narrow and shortsighted imperial policy which places every obstacle in the way of Industrial development and imposes heavy taxes on the struggling people.* According to various authorities, Russia's demand upon landowners in her Central Asian possession are not so exacting as ours in India, *for the British Government insists on a fifth of the produce, making no allowance for good or bad years; while Russia is said to ask only a tenth and allow for variation of production.*" (Pages 135–6, "Russia Against India," by Sir Archibald R. Colquehoun, Gold Medalist, Royal Geographical Society.)

Taxation. Lord Salisbury. The British policy of bleeding Indian people. "The injury is exaggerated in the case of India where so much of the revenue is exported without a direct equivalent. As India must be bled, the lancet should be directed to the parts where the blood is congested or at least sufficient, not to those already feeble for the want of it."—Lord Salisbury.

III

FACTS AND FIGURES

Plague, Deaths from. Plague[1] deaths from 1897–1913: 7,251,257.

Death Rate. Death rate was: 34.28 for the year 1907–11; 32 for the year 1911, and 29.71 for the year 1912.

Rural from 41.8 to 23.5.

Urban from 47.6 to 22.7.

Indian Finance. The budget figures of the government of India for 1914–15 show the total estimated income for the year to be slightly over 85 millions sterling, of which more than 17 millions are given out as railway receipts and about 4½ millions for irrigation work, thus leaving the pure revenue to be about 63 millions.

Land Tax. The principal source of revenue is the land tax, which alone furnishes a little over 21½ millions of pounds, of which, if we deduct 9 millions shown as the "direct demand on the revenues" only 12½ millions are left for general purposes.

The military expenses alone are estimated at about 22 millions, which is even in excess of the gross total receipts from the land tax, and is more than one-third of the total revenues from all sources.

The figures for income are a little misleading, because out of a total of about 17 millions (17 millions and 33 thousand) shown as railway receipts about 13 millions (13,409,000) shown as paid for interest and other miscellaneous charges on the expenditure side, should be deducted. Similarly about 4½ millions are shown as receipts under the head of irrigation, and over 3½ millions are shown against that head as expenditure.

Among the other heads of income, excise brings slightly

[1] We do not mean to say that British Rule in India is responsible for the plague, but with better management of resources, i.e., better sanitation, the plague could have been prevented or eradicated sooner than has been attempted.

over 9 millions. Income tax is included under "Other Heads," which show a total figure of slightly over 5 millions.

Income Tax. The income tax, which is levied on incomes other than those derived from agriculture, is only 6½d. in a pound on incomes of £133 or more, a year, and almost 5d. a pound on incomes below that figure. The minimum taxable income is £66 a year, which shows that all incomes of between 5–6 pounds a month, or between 25–30 dollars a month, are taxed. The large fortunes made by Europeans and Indians by trade, speculation, manufacture, and unearned increments of valuation, are thus easily let off. The principle burden of taxation falls on the poor *ryot.*

Income from agriculture is supposed to be taxed at the rate of 50 per cent. of the net income of the landlord, or at the rate of 20 per cent. of the gross produce of the ryot, under the ryotwari system. In some cases it exceeds these proportions and is as high as 65 per cent. (See Lord Morley's reply to C. T. O'Donnell.)

Customs. Customs, which furnish the principal source of revenue in the United States and Germany, in India only yield about less than 7½ millions. The imports are charged *ad valorem* duty of 5 per cent. with special conditions as to textiles, and "a large free list." The textile woven goods pay a duty of 3½ per cent. and Lancashire is protected by a corresponding excise duty on textile goods produced in the country. Iron and steel pay only a nominal duty of one per cent.

The other principal source of revenue is the drink traffic, from which the government of India makes an income of about *nine millions* sterling. How much loss in morals it inflicts thereby on the country may better be imagined. That however is another story.

TRADE FIGURES FOR 1913 to 1914

Imports (manufactured articles forming 80 per cent. of the total):	£127 millions
Treasure:	29 millions
	£156 millions
Exports (chiefly raw produce and articles of food):	£163 millions

The shipping is entirely in European hands and it would be interesting to enquire how much does India pay for the shipping of its imports and exports, and how much do the foreigners make by way of insurance and other charges. The exact gain to Great Britain and other European countries from Indian trade is simply incalculable. The great bulk of the foreign trade on both sides is in the hands of foreigners.

PERSONNEL OF THE GOVERNMENT

SECRETARY OF STATE and all Under Secretaries, as well as Assistant Under Secretaries:

COUNCIL:	*British*	*British Indians*	*Total*
	8	2	10

All Office Establishment and Secretaries: *British.*

All salaries and other expenses paid by India.

GOVERNOR GENERAL AND COUNCIL *and staff* (i.e., the British Indian Cabinet).

Members of the *Executive Council:* British 7; one only is an Indian.

REVENUE AND AGRICULTURE DEPARTMENT: All Secretaries down to the Superintendent of the Office: British. (Total strength, 7.)

FINANCE DEPARTMENT: 21; all British except that one Assistant Secretary is an Indian, and one Superintendent is an Indian.

FOREIGN DEPARTMENT: 6; all British except that one Attaché is an Indian.

EDUCATION DEPARTMENT: 8; one Assistant Secretary is an Indian.

LEGISLATIVE DEPARTMENT: 7; only one Legal Assistant an Indian.

ARMY DEPARTMENT: 10; one Office Superintendent an Indian.

PUBLIC WORKS: 15; no Indian.

COMMERCE AND INDUSTRY: 11; 3 Office Superintendents are Indians.

RAILWAY BOARD: 4, no Indian.

POST OFFICE AND TELEGRAPH DEPARTMENT: no Indian.

INDO-EUROPEAN TRADE DEPARTMENT: no Indian.

SURVEY: no Indian.

GEOLOGICAL SURVEY: 5; no Indian.

BOTANICAL DEPARTMENT: 5; no Indian.

ARCHÆOLOGICAL SURVEY: 9; one Indian.

MISCELLANEOUS APPOINTMENTS: 39; one Indian.

THE INDIAN LEGISLATIVE COUNCIL:—

Total strength 67, out of which 35, besides the Governor General are always officials, only one of which is an Indian; of the remaining 32, 28 are Indian members, including 3 nominated by the Government, i.e., a total of 20 out of 67.

PROVINCIAL GOVERNMENT:

All Governors, Lieutenant Governors, and Chief Commissioners of Provinces are British.

In Provinces having Executive Councils of three or more, one is an Indian.

Secretaries and Heads of Departments are all Britishers. Of the large army of Under Secretaries and Assistant Secretaries, perhaps one in each Province is an Indian.

SERVICES:

Army: No Indian is eligible to a commissioned rank.

Indian Civil Service: (on the first of April, 1913) out of a total cadre of 1318, only 46 were Indians.

Indian Medical Service: Little over 5 per cent. are Indians.

In Provincial Legislative Councils having very restricted powers of legislation, the *elected* Indians are in a minority everywhere.

FIGURES ABOUT EDUCATION AND LITERACY:

(Figures taken from the Year Book of 1914)

Area, 1,773,168 square miles.
Population, 315,132,537.
Universities in British India, 6.

Number of High Schools for males................1273
Number of High Schools for females............. 144

Primary schools for males 113,955
i.e., not even 1 for every 10 miles.
Primary schools for females................... 13,694

Literally.
Males, 106 per 1000, i.e., about 10½ per cent.
Females, only 10 per 1000, i.e., about 1 per cent.

All these figures are taken from the Indian Year Book, published by the Times of India Press, Bombay, for the years 1914 and 1915.

IV

THE FLOGGING OF POLITICAL PRISONERS

(An extract from *New India*, a paper edited by Mrs. Annie Besant.)

The tragedy of Mr. Ramcharan Lal, the ex-editor of the *Swaraj*, continues. Mr. Macleod, the city magistrate of Nagpur, has sentenced him to an additional six months of rigorous imprisonment after his sentence has expired for 'refusing to work.' Our readers will remember the case. This unfortunate political prisoner — whose analogues in foreign countries have been welcomed and protected on British soil — under-going a sentence of imprisonment, was so brutally flogged for refusing to do work, which he says was more than he could do, that the prison doctor admits that he would have been unable to work for four days after the flogging, and six weeks after it the skin was still discoloured and two serious scars remained. Now he has a heavy sentence of six months' additional imprisonment. Is this British treatment of a political prisoner? Why did Britons protest against the use of the knout on political prisoners in Russia? Is there no one in the House of Commons who will ask a question on this case, and demand an enquiry into the treatment of political prisoners in India?

INDEX